| T | W | T | F | S | S | M | T | W | T | F | S | S | M | T | W | T | F | S | S |
|---|---|---|---|---|---|---|---|---|---|---|---|---|---|---|---|---|---|---|---|
| 17 | 18 | 19 | 20 | 21 | 22 | 23 | 24 | 25 | 26 | 27 | 28 | 29 | 30 | 31 | | | | | |
| 14 | 15 | 16 | 17 | 18 | 19 | 20 | 21 | 22 | 23 | 24 | 25 | 26 | 27 | 28 | | | | | |
| 14 | 15 | 16 | 17 | 18 | 19 | 20 | 21 | 22 | 23 | 24 | 25 | 26 | 27 | 28 | 29 | 30 | 31 | | |
| 18 | 19 | 20 | 21 | 22 | 23 | 24 | 25 | 26 | 27 | 28 | 29 | 30 | | | | | | | |
| 16 | 17 | 18 | 19 | 20 | 21 | 22 | 23 | 24 | 25 | 26 | 27 | 28 | 29 | 30 | 31 | | | | |
| 13 | 14 | 15 | 16 | 17 | 18 | 19 | 20 | 21 | 22 | 23 | 24 | 25 | 26 | 27 | 28 | 29 | 30 | | |
| 18 | 19 | 20 | 21 | 22 | 23 | 24 | 25 | 26 | 27 | 28 | 29 | 30 | 31 | | | | | | |
| 15 | 16 | 17 | 18 | 19 | 20 | 21 | 22 | 23 | 24 | 25 | 26 | 27 | 28 | 29 | 30 | 31 | | | |
| 12 | 13 | 14 | 15 | 16 | 17 | 18 | 19 | 20 | 21 | 22 | 23 | 24 | 25 | 26 | 27 | 28 | 29 | 30 | |
| 17 | 18 | 19 | 20 | 21 | 22 | 23 | 24 | 25 | 26 | 27 | 28 | 29 | 30 | 31 | | | | | |
| 14 | 15 | 16 | 17 | 18 | 19 | 20 | 21 | 22 | 23 | 24 | 25 | 26 | 27 | 28 | 29 | 30 | | | |
| 12 | 13 | 14 | 15 | 16 | 17 | 18 | 19 | 20 | 21 | 22 | 23 | 24 | 25 | 26 | 27 | 28 | 29 | 30 | 31 |

Published by: Haynes Publishing
Sparkford, Yeovil, Somerset BA22 7JJ, UK
Telephone: 01963 440635
International Telephone: +44 1963 440635
Website: www.haynes.co.uk

ISBN 978 1 78521 095 2

Library of Congress Control Number: 2016938861

Haynes North America Inc.,
861 Lawrence Drive, Newbury Park, California 91320, USA

*Whilst every effort has been made to ensure the accuracy of the information
contained within this diary, Haynes Publishing cannot be held responsible for
any errors or omissions.*

Haynes Desk Diary **2017**

# Personal Details

| | |
|---|---|
| Name | |
| Address | |
| | |
| | |
| Postcode | |
| Telephone (Home) | |
| Telephone (Office) | |
| Mobile | |
| Emergency contact | |
| E-mail | |
| National Insurance number | |
| Passport number | |

## Key contact numbers

| | |
|---|---|
| Name | Name |
| Phone | Phone |
| E-mail | E-mail |
| Name | Name |
| Phone | Phone |
| E-mail | E-mail |
| Name | Name |
| Phone | Phone |
| E-mail | E-mail |
| Name | Name |
| Phone | Phone |
| E-mail | E-mail |
| Name | Name |
| Phone | Phone |
| E-mail | E-mail |
| Name | Name |
| Phone | Phone |
| E-mail | E-mail |

# Multifaith Calendar for 2017

*This publication may not include all major religious/cultural holidays.*
*Due to variations in cultural and religious practices and the use of different calendars, some dates of holidays may vary from those listed.*

**Sunday January 1**
Secular
New Year's Day
Shinto
Gantan-sai
Christian Orthodox
Festival of St Basil the Great

**Thursday January 5**
Christian
Twelfth Night
Sikh
Birthday of Guru Gobind Singh

**Friday January 6**
Christian
Epiphany
Christian Armenian Orthodox
Nativity of Christ
Christian Orthodox
Theopany

**Saturday January 7**
Christian Orthodox
Feast of the Nativity

**Sunday January 8**
Christian
Baptism of the Lord

**Saturday January 28**
Chinese
Chinese New Year

**Thursday February 2**
Christian
Candlemas
Pagan
Imbolc

**Friday February 3**
Shinto
Setsebun sai

**Saturday February 11**
Jewish
Tu BiShvat

**Tuesday February 14**
Christian
St Valentine's Day

**Wednesday February 15**
Buddhist
Nirvana day

**Tuesday February 28**
Christian
Shrove Tuesday

**Wednesday March 1**
Christian
St David's Day
Christian
Ash Wednesday

**Thursday March 2**
Bahai
Nineteen Day Fast (start)

**Sunday March 12**
Jewish
Purim
Buddhist
Magha Puja Day

**Monday March 13**
Sikh
Hola Mohalla

**Friday March 17**
Christian
St Patrick's Day

**Sunday March 19**
Christian
St Joseph, husband of the Blessed Virgin Mary

**Tuesday March 21**
Bahai
Naw-Ruz

**Sunday March 26**
Multifaith
Mothering Sunday

**Tuesday March 28**
Hindu
Hindu New Year

**Sunday April 9**
Christian
Palm Sunday

**Tuesday April 11**
Jewish
Passover

**Thursday April 13**
Christian
Maundy Thursday

**Friday April 14**
Christian
Good Friday

**Saturday April 15**
Christian
Easter Saturday

**Sunday April 16**
Christian
Easter
Jewish
Pascha (Easter)

**Monday April 17**
Christian
Easter Monday

**Friday April 21**
Bahai
Ridvan – first day

**Saturday April 23**
Christian
St George's Day

**Saturday April 29**
Jewish
Ridvan – ninth day

**Monday May 1**
Pagan
Beltane

**Tuesday May 2**
Bahai
Ridvan – twelfth day

**Wednesday May 10**
Buddhist
Visakha Puja

**Sunday May 14**
Jewish
Lag B/Omer

**Tuesday May 23**
Christian
Ascension Day

**Thursday May 25**
Baha'i
Declaration of the Bab

**Saturday May 27**
Muslim
Ramadan

**Monday May 29**
Bahai
Ascension of
Baha'u'llah

**Wednesday May 31**
Jewish
Shavuot

**Sunday June 4**
Christian
Pentecost

**Monday June 5**
Christian
Whit Monday

**Sunday June 11**
Christian
Trinity Sunday

**Thursday June 15**
Catholic Christian
Corpus Christi

**Friday June 16**
Sikh
Guru Arjan martyrdom

**Wednesday June 21**
Pagan
Summer Solstice

**Monday June 26**
Islam
Eid al Fitr

**Sunday July 9**
Baha'i
Martyrdom of the Bab

**Saturday July 15**
Christian
St Swithin's Day

**Monday July 24**
Mormon
Pioneer Day

**Tuesday August 1**
Christian
Lammas
Jewish
Tish'a B'av

**Sunday August 6**
Christian
Transfiguration

**Monday August 7**
Hindu
Raksha Bandhan

**Tuesday August 15**
Orthodox Christian
Dormition of the Theotokos
Catholic Christian
Assumption of the Blessed Virgin Mary
Hindu
Krishna Janmashtami

**Friday September 8**
Christian
Birthday of the Blessed Virgin Mary

**Thursday September 14**
Christian
The Triumph of the Cross

**Thursday September 21**
Jewish
Rosh Hashana
Hindu
Navaratri

**Friday September 29**
Christian
Michaelmas/Michael and All Angels

**Saturday September 30**
Jewish
Yom Kippur

**Wednesday October 4**
Christian
Blessing of the Animals
Catholic Christian
St Francis Day

**Thursday October 12**
Jewish
Shemini Atzeret

**Friday October 13**
Jewish
Simchat Torah

**Friday October 20**
Bahai
Birth of the Bab

**Tuesday October 31**
Pagan
Hallowe'en
Christian
Hallowe'en (All Hallows' Eve)

**Wednesday November 1**
Christian
All Saints' Day (Hallowmas, All Hallows')

**Thursday November 2**
Catholic Christian
All Souls Day

**Saturday November 11**
Multifaith
Armistice Day

**Sunday November 12**
Bahai
Birth of Baha'u'llah

**Friday November 24**
Sikh
Martyrdom of Guru Tegh Bahadur

**Sunday November 26**
Bahai
Day of the Covenant

**Tuesday November 28**
Bahai
Ascension of Abdu'l-Baha

**Thursday November 30**
Christian
St Andrew's Day

**Sunday December 3**
Christian
Advent

**Friday December 8**
Catholic
Feast of the Immaculate Conception
Buddhist
Bodhi Day

**Tuesday December 12**
Catholic
Our Lady of Guadeloupe
Muslim
Milad un Nabi (Birthday of the Prophet Muhammad)

**Wednesday December 13**
Jewish
Hanukkah

**Thursday December 21**
Pagan
Winter Solstice

**Sunday December 24**
Christian
Christmas Eve

**Monday December 25**
Christian
Christmas Day
Orthodox Christian
Feast of the Nativity

**Tuesday December 26**
Christian
St Stephen's Day
Secular
Boxing Day

# 2016

## January
| M | T | W | T | F | S | S |
|---|---|---|---|---|---|---|
|  |  |  |  | 1 | **2** | **3** |
| 4 | 5 | 6 | 7 | 8 | **9** | **10** |
| 11 | 12 | 13 | 14 | 15 | **16** | **17** |
| 18 | 19 | 20 | 21 | 22 | **23** | **24** |
| 25 | 26 | 27 | 28 | 29 | **30** | **31** |

## February
| M | T | W | T | F | S | S |
|---|---|---|---|---|---|---|
| 1 | 2 | 3 | 4 | 5 | **6** | **7** |
| 8 | 9 | 10 | 11 | 12 | **13** | **14** |
| 15 | 16 | 17 | 18 | 19 | **20** | **21** |
| 22 | 23 | 24 | 25 | 26 | **27** | **28** |
| 29 |  |  |  |  |  |  |

## March
| M | T | W | T | F | S | S |
|---|---|---|---|---|---|---|
|  | 1 | 2 | 3 | 4 | **5** | **6** |
| 7 | 8 | 9 | 10 | 11 | **12** | **13** |
| 14 | 15 | 16 | 17 | 18 | **19** | **20** |
| 21 | 22 | 23 | 24 | 25 | **26** | **27** |
| 28 | 29 | 30 | 31 |  |  |  |

## April
| M | T | W | T | F | S | S |
|---|---|---|---|---|---|---|
|  |  |  |  | 1 | **2** | **3** |
| 4 | 5 | 6 | 7 | 8 | **9** | **10** |
| 11 | 12 | 13 | 14 | 15 | **16** | **17** |
| 18 | 19 | 20 | 21 | 22 | **23** | **24** |
| 25 | 26 | 27 | 28 | 29 | **30** |  |

## May
| M | T | W | T | F | S | S |
|---|---|---|---|---|---|---|
|  |  |  |  |  |  | **1** |
| 2 | 3 | 4 | 5 | 6 | **7** | **8** |
| 9 | 10 | 11 | 12 | 13 | **14** | **15** |
| 16 | 17 | 18 | 19 | 20 | **21** | **22** |
| 23 | 24 | 25 | 26 | 27 | **28** | **29** |
| 30 | 31 |  |  |  |  |  |

## June
| M | T | W | T | F | S | S |
|---|---|---|---|---|---|---|
|  |  | 1 | 2 | 3 | **4** | **5** |
| 6 | 7 | 8 | 9 | 10 | **11** | **12** |
| 13 | 14 | 15 | 16 | 17 | **18** | **19** |
| 20 | 21 | 22 | 23 | 24 | **25** | **26** |
| 27 | 28 | 29 | 30 |  |  |  |

## July
| M | T | W | T | F | S | S |
|---|---|---|---|---|---|---|
|  |  |  |  | 1 | **2** | **3** |
| 4 | 5 | 6 | 7 | 8 | **9** | **10** |
| 11 | 12 | 13 | 14 | 15 | **16** | **17** |
| 18 | 19 | 20 | 21 | 22 | **23** | **24** |
| 25 | 26 | 27 | 28 | 29 | **30** | **31** |

## August
| M | T | W | T | F | S | S |
|---|---|---|---|---|---|---|
| 1 | 2 | 3 | 4 | 5 | **6** | **7** |
| 8 | 9 | 10 | 11 | 12 | **13** | **14** |
| 15 | 16 | 17 | 18 | 19 | **20** | **21** |
| 22 | 23 | 24 | 25 | 26 | **27** | **28** |
| 29 | 30 | 31 |  |  |  |  |

## September
| M | T | W | T | F | S | S |
|---|---|---|---|---|---|---|
|  |  |  | 1 | 2 | **3** | **4** |
| 5 | 6 | 7 | 8 | 9 | **10** | **11** |
| 12 | 13 | 14 | 15 | 16 | **17** | **18** |
| 19 | 20 | 21 | 22 | 23 | **24** | **25** |
| 26 | 27 | 28 | 29 | 30 |  |  |

## October
| M | T | W | T | F | S | S |
|---|---|---|---|---|---|---|
|  |  |  |  |  | **1** | **2** |
| 3 | 4 | 5 | 6 | 7 | **8** | **9** |
| 10 | 11 | 12 | 13 | 14 | **15** | **16** |
| 17 | 18 | 19 | 20 | 21 | **22** | **23** |
| 24 | 25 | 26 | 27 | 28 | **29** | **30** |
| 31 |  |  |  |  |  |  |

## November
| M | T | W | T | F | S | S |
|---|---|---|---|---|---|---|
|  | 1 | 2 | 3 | 4 | **5** | **6** |
| 7 | 8 | 9 | 10 | 11 | **12** | **13** |
| 14 | 15 | 16 | 17 | 18 | **19** | **20** |
| 21 | 22 | 23 | 24 | 25 | **26** | **27** |
| 28 | 29 | 30 |  |  |  |  |

## December
| M | T | W | T | F | S | S |
|---|---|---|---|---|---|---|
|  |  |  | 1 | 2 | **3** | **4** |
| 5 | 6 | 7 | 8 | 9 | **10** | **11** |
| 12 | 13 | 14 | 15 | 16 | **17** | **18** |
| 19 | 20 | 21 | 22 | 23 | **24** | **25** |
| 26 | 27 | 28 | 29 | 30 | 31 |  |

# 2017

## January
| M | T | W | T | F | S | S |
|---|---|---|---|---|---|---|
|  |  |  |  |  |  | **1** |
| 2 | 3 | 4 | 5 | 6 | **7** | **8** |
| 9 | 10 | 11 | 12 | 13 | **14** | **15** |
| 16 | 17 | 18 | 19 | 20 | **21** | **22** |
| 23 | 24 | 25 | 26 | 27 | **28** | **29** |
| 30 | 31 |  |  |  |  |  |

## February
| M | T | W | T | F | S | S |
|---|---|---|---|---|---|---|
|  |  | 1 | 2 | 3 | **4** | **5** |
| 6 | 7 | 8 | 9 | 10 | **11** | **12** |
| 13 | 14 | 15 | 16 | 17 | **18** | **19** |
| 20 | 21 | 22 | 23 | 24 | **25** | **26** |
| 27 | 28 |  |  |  |  |  |

## March
| M | T | W | T | F | S | S |
|---|---|---|---|---|---|---|
|  |  | 1 | 2 | 3 | **4** | **5** |
| 6 | 7 | 8 | 9 | 10 | **11** | **12** |
| 13 | 14 | 15 | 16 | 17 | **18** | **19** |
| 20 | 21 | 22 | 23 | 24 | **25** | **26** |
| 27 | 28 | 29 | 30 | 31 |  |  |

## April
| M | T | W | T | F | S | S |
|---|---|---|---|---|---|---|
|  |  |  |  |  | **1** | **2** |
| 3 | 4 | 5 | 6 | 7 | **8** | **9** |
| 10 | 11 | 12 | 13 | 14 | **15** | **16** |
| 17 | 18 | 19 | 20 | 21 | **22** | **23** |
| 24 | 25 | 26 | 27 | 28 | **29** | **30** |

## May
| M | T | W | T | F | S | S |
|---|---|---|---|---|---|---|
| 1 | 2 | 3 | 4 | 5 | **6** | **7** |
| 8 | 9 | 10 | 11 | 12 | **13** | **14** |
| 15 | 16 | 17 | 18 | 19 | **20** | **21** |
| 22 | 23 | 24 | 25 | 26 | **27** | **28** |
| 29 | 30 | 31 |  |  |  |  |

## June
| M | T | W | T | F | S | S |
|---|---|---|---|---|---|---|
|  |  |  | 1 | 2 | **3** | **4** |
| 5 | 6 | 7 | 8 | 9 | **10** | **11** |
| 12 | 13 | 14 | 15 | 16 | **17** | **18** |
| 19 | 20 | 21 | 22 | 23 | **24** | **25** |
| 26 | 27 | 28 | 29 | 30 |  |  |

## July
| M | T | W | T | F | S | S |
|---|---|---|---|---|---|---|
|  |  |  |  |  | **1** | **2** |
| 3 | 4 | 5 | 6 | 7 | **8** | **9** |
| 10 | 11 | 12 | 13 | 14 | **15** | **16** |
| 17 | 18 | 19 | 20 | 21 | **22** | **23** |
| 24 | 25 | 26 | 27 | 28 | **29** | **30** |
| 31 |  |  |  |  |  |  |

## August
| M | T | W | T | F | S | S |
|---|---|---|---|---|---|---|
|  | 1 | 2 | 3 | 4 | **5** | **6** |
| 7 | 8 | 9 | 10 | 11 | **12** | **13** |
| 14 | 15 | 16 | 17 | 18 | **19** | **20** |
| 21 | 22 | 23 | 24 | 25 | **26** | **27** |
| 28 | 29 | 30 | 31 |  |  |  |

## September
| M | T | W | T | F | S | S |
|---|---|---|---|---|---|---|
|  |  |  |  | 1 | **2** | **3** |
| 4 | 5 | 6 | 7 | 8 | **9** | **10** |
| 11 | 12 | 13 | 14 | 15 | **16** | **17** |
| 18 | 19 | 20 | 21 | 22 | **23** | **24** |
| 25 | 26 | 27 | 28 | 29 | **30** |  |

## October
| M | T | W | T | F | S | S |
|---|---|---|---|---|---|---|
|  |  |  |  |  |  | **1** |
| 2 | 3 | 4 | 5 | 6 | **7** | **8** |
| 9 | 10 | 11 | 12 | 13 | **14** | **15** |
| 16 | 17 | 18 | 19 | 20 | **21** | **22** |
| 23 | 24 | 25 | 26 | 27 | **28** | **29** |
| 30 | 31 |  |  |  |  |  |

## November
| M | T | W | T | F | S | S |
|---|---|---|---|---|---|---|
|  |  | 1 | 2 | 3 | **4** | **5** |
| 6 | 7 | 8 | 9 | 10 | **11** | **12** |
| 13 | 14 | 15 | 16 | 17 | **18** | **19** |
| 20 | 21 | 22 | 23 | 24 | **25** | **26** |
| 27 | 28 | 29 | 30 |  |  |  |

## December
| M | T | W | T | F | S | S |
|---|---|---|---|---|---|---|
|  |  |  |  | 1 | **2** | **3** |
| 4 | 5 | 6 | 7 | 8 | **9** | **10** |
| 11 | 12 | 13 | 14 | 15 | **16** | **17** |
| 18 | 19 | 20 | 21 | 22 | **23** | **24** |
| 25 | 26 | 27 | 28 | 29 | **30** | **31** |

# 2018

## January
| M | T | W | T | F | S | S |
|---|---|---|---|---|---|---|
| 1 | 2 | 3 | 4 | 5 | **6** | **7** |
| 8 | 9 | 10 | 11 | 12 | **13** | **14** |
| 15 | 16 | 17 | 18 | 19 | **20** | **21** |
| 22 | 23 | 24 | 25 | 26 | **27** | **28** |
| 29 | 30 | 31 |  |  |  |  |

## February
| M | T | W | T | F | S | S |
|---|---|---|---|---|---|---|
|  |  |  | 1 | 2 | **3** | **4** |
| 5 | 6 | 7 | 8 | 9 | **10** | **11** |
| 12 | 13 | 14 | 15 | 16 | **17** | **18** |
| 19 | 20 | 21 | 22 | 23 | **24** | **25** |
| 26 | 27 | 28 |  |  |  |  |

## March
| M | T | W | T | F | S | S |
|---|---|---|---|---|---|---|
|  |  |  | 1 | 2 | **3** | **4** |
| 5 | 6 | 7 | 8 | 9 | **10** | **11** |
| 12 | 13 | 14 | 15 | 16 | **17** | **18** |
| 19 | 20 | 21 | 22 | 23 | **24** | **25** |
| 26 | 27 | 28 | 29 | 30 | **31** |  |

## April
| M | T | W | T | F | S | S |
|---|---|---|---|---|---|---|
|  |  |  |  |  |  | **1** |
| 2 | 3 | 4 | 5 | 6 | **7** | **8** |
| 9 | 10 | 11 | 12 | 13 | **14** | **15** |
| 16 | 17 | 18 | 19 | 20 | **21** | **22** |
| 23 | 24 | 25 | 26 | 27 | **28** | **29** |
| 30 |  |  |  |  |  |  |

## May
| M | T | W | T | F | S | S |
|---|---|---|---|---|---|---|
|  | 1 | 2 | 3 | 4 | **5** | **6** |
| 7 | 8 | 9 | 10 | 11 | **12** | **13** |
| 14 | 15 | 16 | 17 | 18 | **19** | **20** |
| 21 | 22 | 23 | 24 | 25 | **26** | **27** |
| 28 | 29 | 30 | 31 |  |  |  |

## June
| M | T | W | T | F | S | S |
|---|---|---|---|---|---|---|
|  |  |  |  | 1 | **2** | **3** |
| 4 | 5 | 6 | 7 | 8 | **9** | **10** |
| 11 | 12 | 13 | 14 | 15 | **16** | **17** |
| 18 | 19 | 20 | 21 | 22 | **23** | **24** |
| 25 | 26 | 27 | 28 | 29 | **30** |  |

## July
| M | T | W | T | F | S | S |
|---|---|---|---|---|---|---|
|  |  |  |  |  |  | **1** |
| 2 | 3 | 4 | 5 | 6 | **7** | **8** |
| 9 | 10 | 11 | 12 | 13 | **14** | **15** |
| 16 | 17 | 18 | 19 | 20 | **21** | **22** |
| 23 | 24 | 25 | 26 | 27 | **28** | **29** |
| 30 | 31 |  |  |  |  |  |

## August
| M | T | W | T | F | S | S |
|---|---|---|---|---|---|---|
|  |  | 1 | 2 | 3 | **4** | **5** |
| 6 | 7 | 8 | 9 | 10 | **11** | **12** |
| 13 | 14 | 15 | 16 | 17 | **18** | **19** |
| 20 | 21 | 22 | 23 | 24 | **25** | **26** |
| 27 | 28 | 29 | 30 | 31 |  |  |

## September
| M | T | W | T | F | S | S |
|---|---|---|---|---|---|---|
|  |  |  |  |  | **1** | **2** |
| 3 | 4 | 5 | 6 | 7 | **8** | **9** |
| 10 | 11 | 12 | 13 | 14 | **15** | **16** |
| 17 | 18 | 19 | 20 | 21 | **22** | **23** |
| 24 | 25 | 26 | 27 | 28 | **29** | **30** |

## October
| M | T | W | T | F | S | S |
|---|---|---|---|---|---|---|
| 1 | 2 | 3 | 4 | 5 | **6** | **7** |
| 8 | 9 | 10 | 11 | 12 | **13** | **14** |
| 15 | 16 | 17 | 18 | 19 | **20** | **21** |
| 22 | 23 | 24 | 25 | 26 | **27** | **28** |
| 29 | 30 | 31 |  |  |  |  |

## November
| M | T | W | T | F | S | S |
|---|---|---|---|---|---|---|
|  |  |  | 1 | 2 | **3** | **4** |
| 5 | 6 | 7 | 8 | 9 | **10** | **11** |
| 12 | 13 | 14 | 15 | 16 | **17** | **18** |
| 19 | 20 | 21 | 22 | 23 | **24** | **25** |
| 26 | 27 | 28 | 29 | 30 |  |  |

## December
| M | T | W | T | F | S | S |
|---|---|---|---|---|---|---|
|  |  |  |  |  | **1** | **2** |
| 3 | 4 | 5 | 6 | 7 | **8** | **9** |
| 10 | 11 | 12 | 13 | 14 | **15** | **16** |
| 17 | 18 | 19 | 20 | 21 | **22** | **23** |
| 24 | 25 | 26 | 27 | 28 | **29** | **30** |
| 31 |  |  |  |  |  |  |

**19** **Monday**

**20** **Tuesday**

**21** **Wednesday**                                    Winter Solstice (shortest day)

## 22 Thursday

## 23 Friday

## 24 Saturday

Christmas Eve

## 25 Sunday

Christmas Day

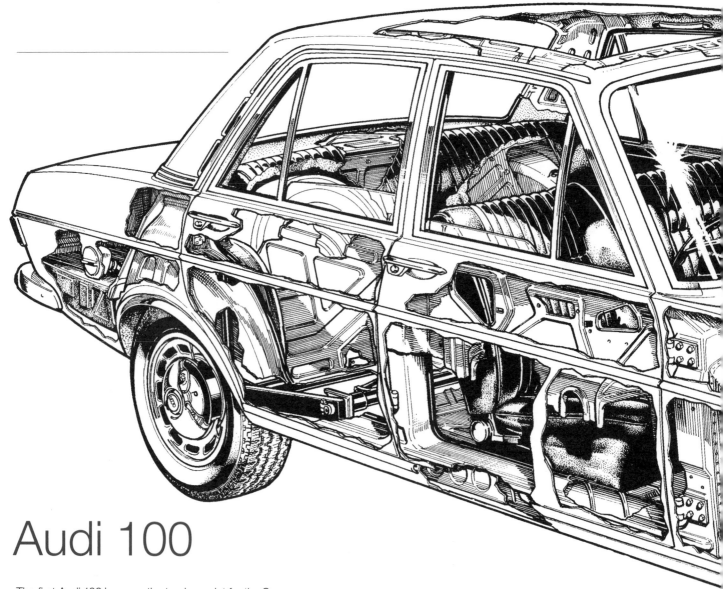

# Audi 100

The first Audi 100 became the turning point for the German marque, as it was the first Audi to directly challenge the premium executive car sector that was previously the preserve of Rover, Ford and BMW. What's more, it was technically more advanced than most large saloons, boasting front-wheel drive with in-line engines.

Auto Union, the Audi parent company, had been sold by Daimler-Benz to Volkswagen in 1965, and gifted with it was the Audi 100 design which had enjoyed plenty of input from Mercedes' quality-obsessed development engineers. VW, however, mainly wanted to get its hands on Auto Union's Ingolstadt factory to boost production of its own Beetle, and postponed all new Audis while the facilities were absorbed. Even

though he was forbidden from working on the car, the 100's father Ludwig Kraus went on refining it and, when VW boss Heinrich Nordhoff saw the excellent result, with its sleek styling, he changed his mind and gave the car the green light.

From this single decision sprang the entire growth of Audi as a leading sports and luxury brand. Also, in introducing a thoroughly-developed water-cooled design to Volkswagen, it helped pave the way, via the VW K70 and Passat, for the Volkswagen revolution that did away with the air-cooled, rear-engined Beetle and ushered in the excellent Golf. So admire this motor car's fine features, and salute its pioneer status!

## Month **Planner**

| Sunday | Monday | Tuesday | Wednesday | Thursday | Friday | Saturday | Sunday | Monday | Tuesday | Wednesday | Thursday | Friday | Saturday | Sunday | Monday |
|--------|--------|---------|-----------|----------|--------|----------|--------|--------|---------|-----------|----------|--------|----------|--------|--------|
| 1 | 2 | 3 | 4 | 5 | 6 | 7 | 8 | 9 | 10 | 11 | 12 | 13 | 14 | 15 | 16 |

| Tuesday | Wednesday | Thursday | Friday | Saturday | Sunday | Monday | Tuesday | Wednesday | Thursday | Friday | Saturday | Sunday | Monday | `Tuesday |
|---|---|---|---|---|---|---|---|---|---|---|---|---|---|---|
| 17 | 18 | 19 | 20 | 21 | 22 | 23 | 24 | 25 | 26 | 27 | 28 | 29 | 30 | 31 |

**26** **Monday** Boxing Day (Bank Holiday)

**27** **Tuesday**

**28** **Wednesday**

## 29 **Thursday**

## 30 **Friday**

## 31 **Saturday**                                     New Year's Eve

## 1 **Sunday**                                        New Year's Day

**2** **Monday**

**3** **Tuesday**

**4** **Wednesday**

**5** **Thursday**

**6** **Friday**

**7** **Saturday**

**8** **Sunday**

## 9 **Monday**

## 10 **Tuesday**

## 11 **Wednesday**

## 12 **Thursday**

## 13 **Friday**

## 14 **Saturday**

## 15 **Sunday**

**16** **Monday**

**17** **Tuesday**

**18** **Wednesday**

# 19 **Thursday**

# 20 **Friday**

# 21 **Saturday**

# 22 **Sunday**

JAN

**23** **Monday**

**24** **Tuesday**

**25** **Wednesday**

**26** **Thursday**

**27** **Friday**

**28** **Saturday**

**29** **Sunday**

# February 2017

## Soyuz

A product of the Cold War and the space race that saw Russia and the United States struggling to put the first men on the Moon, the Soyuz spacecraft was designed in the early 1960s and has been carrying cosmonauts and astronauts into orbit for almost 50 years. In that time it has served to deliver people to several Soviet-era space stations and to the International Space Station (ISS) since 2000, when it carried the Expedition 1 crew to the orbiting facility.

Throughout the assembly phase of the ISS, Soyuz stood in as the sole means of humans reaching space on occasions when the Shuttle was grounded. This occurred after the loss of *Columbia* in 2004, and since 2011 when the Shuttle was retired. Soyuz is likely to remain the sole means for anyone from Earth being able to access space for several years.

The evolution of Soyuz began with its origin as successor to the Vostok-era capsules which carried early cosmonauts into space, then through the Zond spacecraft which aimed to send humans to the Moon and back, and to the unmanned Progress cargo-tanker vehicles which serviced space stations with goods and supplies. In late 2015, Tim Peake launched into space aboard a Soyuz spacecraft to become Britain's first official astronaut on board the International Space Station.

Soyuz has proven to be the most versatile spacecraft ever built, serving many roles across five decades.

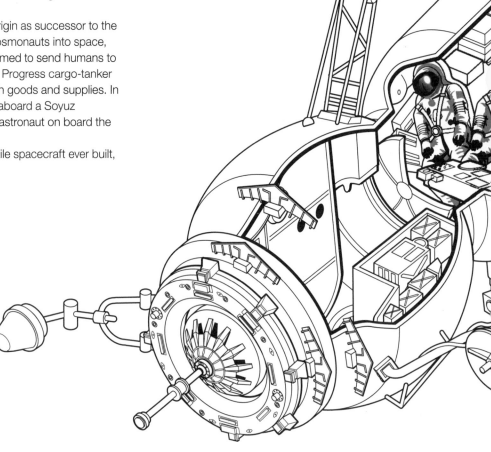

## Month **Planner**

| Wednesday | Thursday | Friday | Saturday | Sunday | Monday | Tuesday | Wednesday | Thursday | Friday | Saturday | Sunday | Monday | Tuesday | Wednesday | Thursday |
|---|---|---|---|---|---|---|---|---|---|---|---|---|---|---|---|
| 1 | 2 | 3 | 4 | 5 | 6 | 7 | 8 | 9 | 10 | 11 | 12 | 13 | 14 | 15 | 16 |

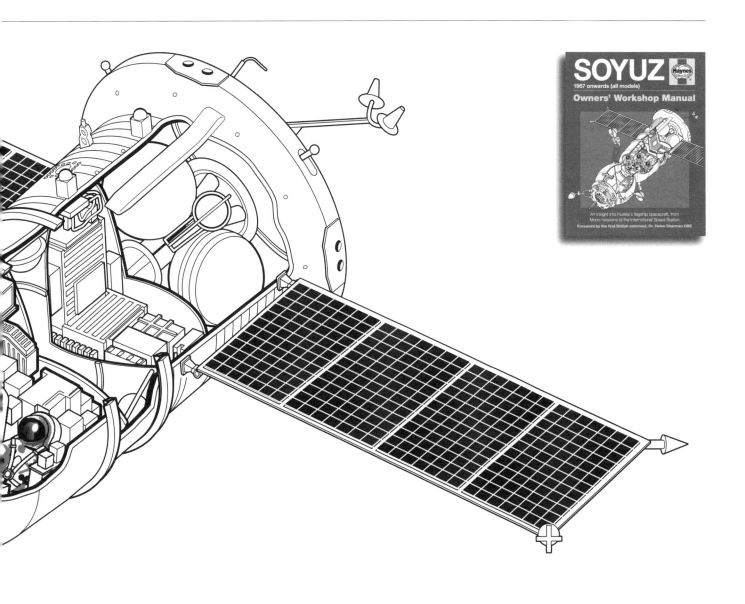

| Friday | Saturday | Sunday | Monday | Tuesday | Wednesday | Thursday | Friday | Saturday | Sunday | Monday | Tuesday |
|--------|----------|--------|--------|---------|-----------|----------|--------|----------|--------|--------|---------|
| 17 | 18 | 19 | 20 | 21 | 22 | 23 | 24 | 25 | 26 | 27 | 28 |

## 30 Monday

## 31 Tuesday

## 1 Wednesday

## 2 Thursday

## 3 Friday

## 4 Saturday

## 5 Sunday

6 **Monday**

7 **Tuesday**

8 **Wednesday**

## 9 Thursday

## 10 Friday

## 11 Saturday

## 12 Sunday

# **February** 2017

**13** **Monday**

**14** **Tuesday**                                                    St Valentine's Day

**15** **Wednesday**

**16** **Thursday**

**17** **Friday**

**18** **Saturday**

**19** **Sunday**

FEB

**20** **Monday**

**21** **Tuesday**

**22** **Wednesday**

**23** Thursday

**24** Friday

**25** Saturday

**26** Sunday

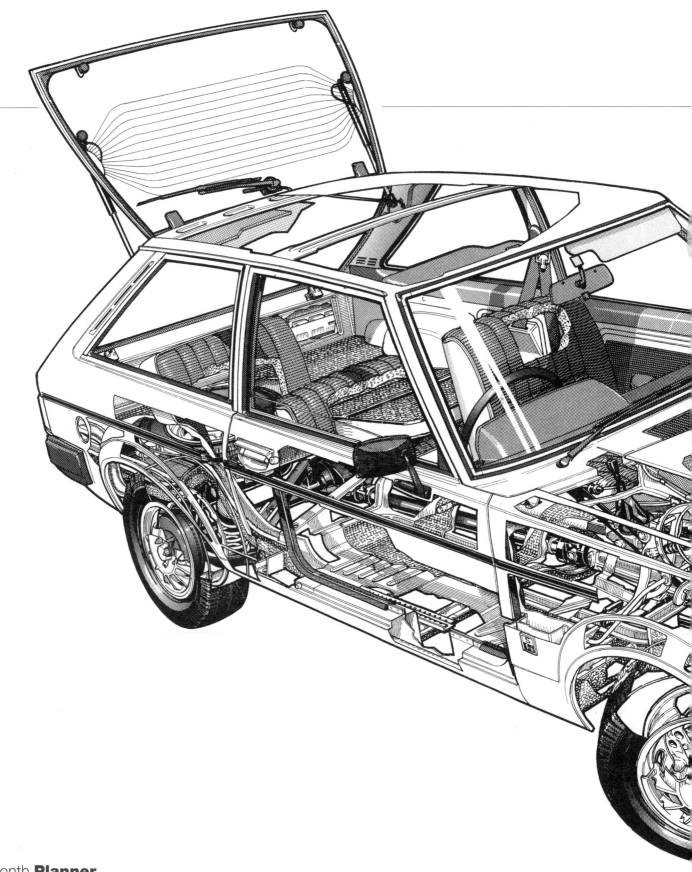

## Month **Planner**

| Wednesday | Thursday | Friday | Saturday | Sunday | Monday | Tuesday | Wednesday | Thursday | Friday | Saturday | Sunday | Monday | Tuesday | Wednesday | Thursday |
|---|---|---|---|---|---|---|---|---|---|---|---|---|---|---|---|
| 1 | 2 | 3 | 4 | 5 | 6 | 7 | 8 | 9 | 10 | 11 | 12 | 13 | 14 | 15 | 16 |

# Chrysler Sunbeam

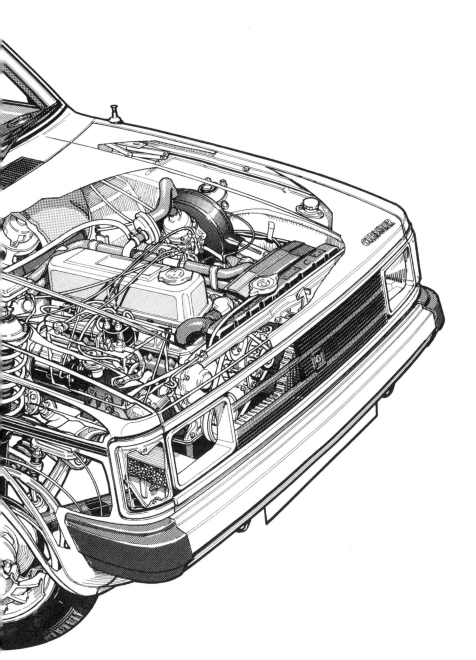

The Sunbeam was born of a political storm and ended up a rallying hero. The rallying bit occurred after Henri Toivonen took it to victory in the 1980 Lombard RAC Rally, and Sunbeam Lotus subsequently clinched the 1981 Manufacturers' Championship for its builder. The rear-wheel-drive balance may have been good for the circuits, but it had its roots in the Hillman/Chrysler Avenger.

The Sunbeam was created, in a mere 19 months, as Chrysler UK's side of a bargain struck with the British government. In return for state aid to bolster the ailing company, Chrysler agreed to design a new small car to build at its Linwood, Scotland, plant, using as many British-made components as possible.

So the Avenger was shortened, given a neat two-box body with an opening glass tailgate (engineering a proper hatchback into the existing structure was too costly), and an engine line-up that included 1.3- and 1.6-litre Avenger units and the 1-litre aluminium engine formerly used in the Hillman Imp.

A lash-up? Actually, the Sunbeam was a decent enough small car with a simple mechanical layout. It was certainly capable of spawning two 'hot' versions: a twin-carburettor Ti, and the beefed-up Lotus-built special with its 16-valve, 150bhp 2.2-litre engine and ZF five-speed gearbox. Only… this ultimate Sunbeam hit the market in 1980, by when all European-built Chryslers had been renamed Talbots.

| Friday | Saturday | Sunday | Monday | Tuesday | Wednesday | Thursday | Friday | Saturday | Sunday | Monday | Tuesday | Wednesday | Thursday | Friday |
|---|---|---|---|---|---|---|---|---|---|---|---|---|---|---|
| 17 | 18 | 19 | 20 | 21 | 22 | 23 | 24 | 25 | 26 | 27 | 28 | 29 | 30 | 31 |

# February/March 2017

## 27 Monday

## 28 Tuesday
Shrove Tuesday

## 1 Wednesday
Ash Wednesday
St David's Day (Wales)

## 2 Thursday

## 3 Friday

## 4 Saturday

## 5 Sunday

6 **Monday**

7 **Tuesday**

8 **Wednesday**

## 9 Thursday

## 10 Friday

## 11 Saturday

## 12 Sunday

MAR

**13** **Monday**

MAR

**14** **Tuesday**

**15** **Wednesday**

**16** **Thursday**

**17** **Friday**                                                   St Patrick's Day (Ireland)

**18** **Saturday**

**19** **Sunday**

**20** **Monday** Spring Equinox

**21** **Tuesday**

**22** **Wednesday**

MAR

**23** **Thursday**

**24** **Friday**

**25** **Saturday**

**26** **Sunday**

British Summer Time begins
Mothering Sunday (UK)

# April 2017

## Norton Commando

The first Commando was introduced in 1968 with a 745cc vertical twin engine derived from the Dominator and Atlas range. The feature which set the Commando apart from its predecessors was the Norton-Villiers patented Isolastic suspension mountings which eliminated the high level frequency vibration inherent in vertical twins. The 750 model range included the Fastback, S, Roadster, Hi-Rider, Interstate and John Player production racer, plus there was the Interpol model built for Police use. A higher spec 'Combat' engine was available producing 65bhp, 5 bhp more than the standard engine. Later 750s were fitted with a front disc brake, as on the Roadster shown.

In 1973 the Commando's engine was beefed up and capacity increased to 828cc by enlarging bore diameter. Further improvements were made two years later on the Mk 3 in the fitting of electric start, rear disc brake (front disc now relocated to left side of hub) and adjustable engine mountings, plus the switch to a left side gearchange and right side rear brake to suit the US market.

Norton was no stranger to TT success, but it was employee and factory rider Peter Williams who took a JPS Commando to victory in the Formula 750 at the 1973 IoM TT.

Production of the last Commando, the Mk III Interstate 850, came to an end in 1978.

## Month **Planner**

| Saturday | Sunday | Monday | Tuesday | Wednesday | Thursday | Friday | Saturday | Sunday | Monday | Tuesday | Wednesday | Thursday | Friday | Saturday | Sunday |
|---|---|---|---|---|---|---|---|---|---|---|---|---|---|---|---|
| 1 | 2 | 3 | 4 | 5 | 6 | 7 | 8 | 9 | 10 | 11 | 12 | 13 | 14 | 15 | 16 |

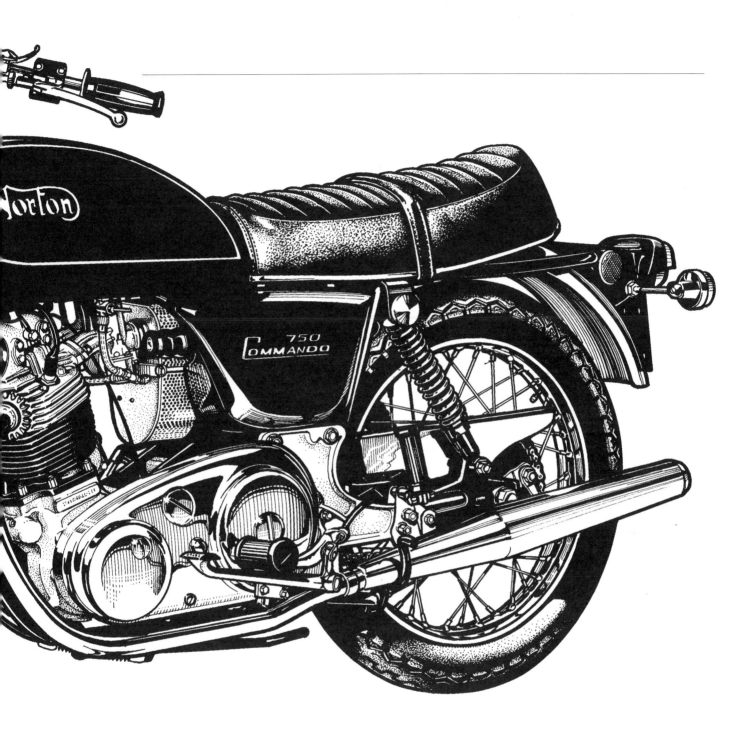

| Monday | Tuesday | Wednesday | Thursday | Friday | Saturday | Sunday | Monday | Tuesday | Wednesday | Thursday | Friday | Saturday | Sunday |
|--------|---------|-----------|----------|--------|----------|--------|--------|---------|-----------|----------|--------|----------|--------|
| 17 | 18 | 19 | 20 | 21 | 22 | 23 | 24 | 25 | 26 | 27 | 28 | 29 | 30 |

MAR

**27** **Monday**

**28** **Tuesday**

**29** **Wednesday**

**30** | **Thursday**

**31** | **Friday**

**1** | **Saturday**

**2** | **Sunday**

**3** **Monday**

**4** **Tuesday**

**5** **Wednesday**

**6** **Thursday**

**7** **Friday**

**8** **Saturday**

**9** **Sunday**                                                     Palm Sunday

10 **Monday**

11 **Tuesday**

12 **Wednesday**

## 13 **Thursday**

Maundy Thursday

## 14 **Friday**

Good Friday Bank Holiday

## 15 **Saturday**

## 16 **Sunday**

Easter Sunday

## 17 **Monday**

Easter Monday Bank Holiday (not Scotland)

## 18 **Tuesday**

## 19 **Wednesday**

## 20 Thursday

## 21 Friday

## 22 Saturday

## 23 Sunday

St George's Day (England)

24 **Monday**

25 **Tuesday**

26 **Wednesday**

**27** **Thursday**

**28** **Friday**

**29** **Saturday**

**30** **Sunday**

# May 2017

# Ford Prefect

If you were after typical Ford dependability in compact four-door form during the 1950s then this was the car for you. However, like the bigger Consul and Zephyr models, the Prefect was a modern design with integral monocoque construction and the MacPherson strut front suspension that those bigger Fords had pioneered.

Where the 100E Prefect was a bit dated was in its engine department, where the faithful sidevalve 1,172cc engine held sway. Neither very fuel-efficient nor that lively, this little lump did at least offer technical simplicity and few maintenance headaches. A three-speed gearbox reflected the Prefect's limited aspirations towards vivid acceleration, although the hydraulic brakes were a massive improvement over the feeble mechanical items in the previous 'sit-up-and-beg' Prefect.

The 100E range, of course, also included the two-door Popular and Escort estate. Apart from its four doors, the Prefect was immediately distinguishable from its little brother thanks to its vertical grille bars. Its estate twin the two-door Squire shared the Prefect's convex frontage.

There were major changes in store for the Prefect in 1959. Ford installed the all-new, overhead-valve 997cc engine from the all-new 105E Anglia. Despite its smaller capacity, it transformed the Prefect's performance, which could be fully exploited thanks to an Anglia four-speed gearbox. Known as the 107E series, it survived until 1961 and was sold only in natty two-tone paint schemes.

## Month **Planner**

| Monday | Tuesday | Wednesday | Thursday | Friday | Saturday | Sunday | Monday | Tuesday | Wednesday | Thursday | Friday | Saturday | Sunday | Monday | Tuesday |
|---|---|---|---|---|---|---|---|---|---|---|---|---|---|---|---|
| 1 | 2 | 3 | 4 | 5 | 6 | 7 | 8 | 9 | 10 | 11 | 12 | 13 | 14 | 15 | 16 |

| Wednesday | Thursday | Friday | Saturday | Sunday | Monday | Tuesday | Wednesday | Thursday | Friday | Saturday | Sunday | Monday | Tuesday | Wednesday |
|-----------|----------|--------|----------|--------|--------|---------|-----------|----------|--------|----------|--------|--------|----------|-----------|
| 17 | 18 | 19 | 20 | 21 | 22 | 23 | 24 | 25 | 26 | 27 | 28 | 29 | 30 | 31 |

## 1 Monday

May Day Bank Holiday

## 2 Tuesday

## 3 Wednesday

4 **Thursday**

5 **Friday**

6 **Saturday**

7 **Sunday**

**8** **Monday**

**9** **Tuesday**

**10** **Wednesday**

## 11 **Thursday**

## 12 **Friday**

## 13 **Saturday**

## 14 **Sunday**

## 15 Monday

## 16 Tuesday

## 17 Wednesday

## 18 Thursday

## 19 Friday

## 20 Saturday

## 21 Sunday

22 **Monday**

23 **Tuesday**

24 **Wednesday**

## 25 Thursday

## 26 Friday

## 27 Saturday

## 28 Sunday

# June 2017

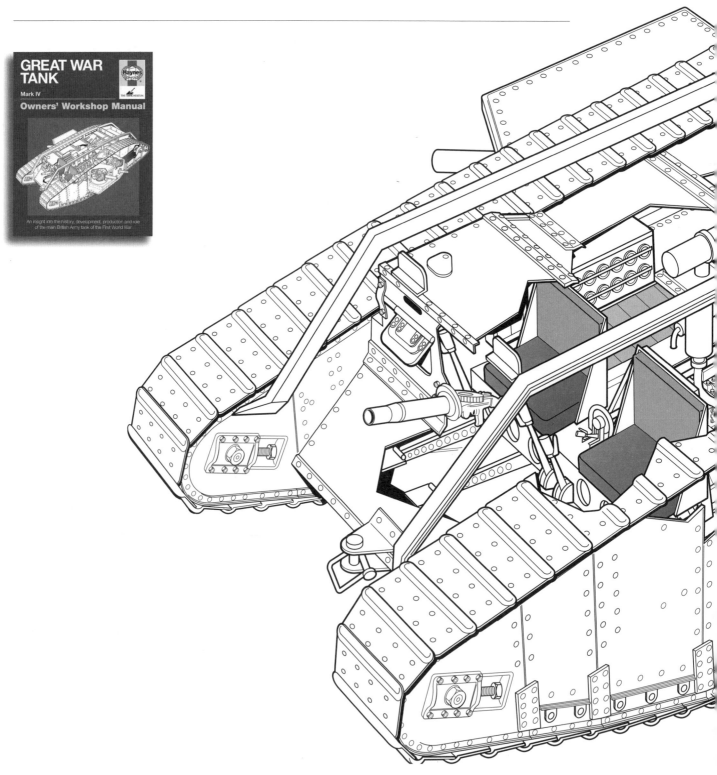

GREAT WAR
TANK
Mark IV
Owners' Workshop Manual

An insight into the history, development, production and role
of the main British Army tank of the First World War

## Month **Planner**

| *Thursday | Friday | Saturday | Sunday | Monday | Tuesday | Wednesday | Thursday | Friday | Saturday | Sunday | Monday | Tuesday | Wednesday | Thursday | Friday |
|---|---|---|---|---|---|---|---|---|---|---|---|---|---|---|---|
| 1 | 2 | 3 | 4 | 5 | 6 | 7 | 8 | 9 | 10 | 11 | 12 | 13 | 14 | 15 | 16 |

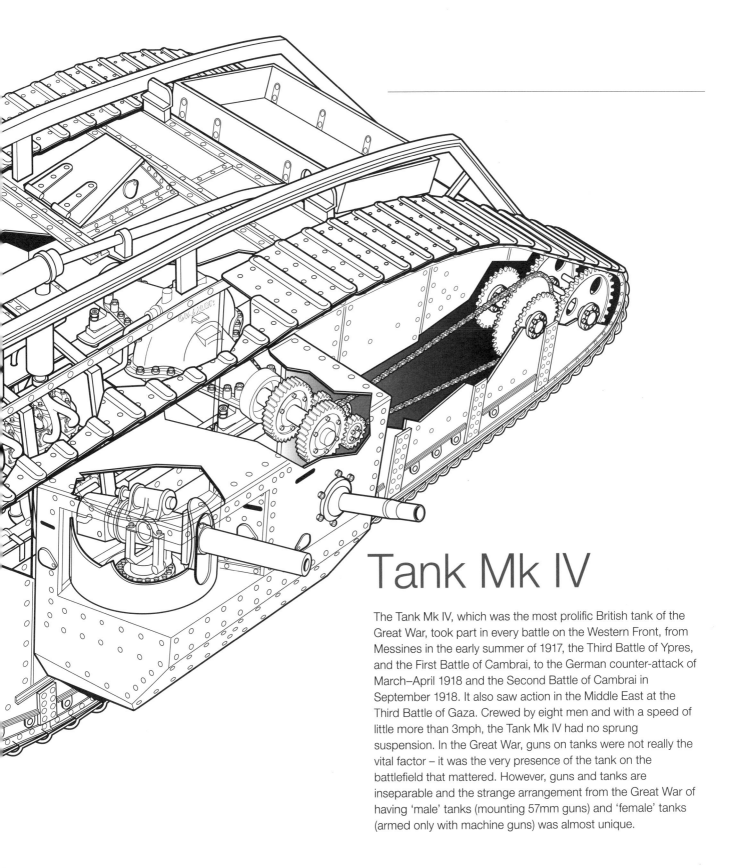

# Tank Mk IV

The Tank Mk IV, which was the most prolific British tank of the
Great War, took part in every battle on the Western Front, from
Messines in the early summer of 1917, the Third Battle of Ypres,
and the First Battle of Cambrai, to the German counter-attack of
March–April 1918 and the Second Battle of Cambrai in
September 1918. It also saw action in the Middle East at the
Third Battle of Gaza. Crewed by eight men and with a speed of
little more than 3mph, the Tank Mk IV had no sprung
suspension. In the Great War, guns on tanks were not really the
vital factor – it was the very presence of the tank on the
battlefield that mattered. However, guns and tanks are
inseparable and the strange arrangement from the Great War of
having 'male' tanks (mounting 57mm guns) and 'female' tanks
(armed only with machine guns) was almost unique.

| Saturday | Sunday | Monday | Tuesday | Wednesday | Thursday | Friday | Saturday | Sunday | Monday | Tuesdsay | Wednesday | Thursday | Friday |
|---|---|---|---|---|---|---|---|---|---|---|---|---|---|
| 17 | 18 | 19 | 20 | 21 | 22 | 23 | 24 | 25 | 26 | 27 | 28 | 29 | 30 |

**29** **Monday**                                                    Spring Bank Holiday

**30** **Tuesday**

MAY

**31** **Wednesday**

**1** **Thursday**

**2** **Friday**

**3** **Saturday**

**4** **Sunday**

5 **Monday**

6 **Tuesday**

7 **Wednesday**

**8** **Thursday**

**9** **Friday**

**10** **Saturday**

**11** **Sunday**

**12** **Monday**

**13** **Tuesday**

**14** **Wednesday**

**15** | **Thursday**

**16** | **Friday**

**17** | **Saturday**

**18** | **Sunday**                                        Father's Day (UK)

**19** **Monday**

**JUN**

**20** **Tuesday**

**21** **Wednesday**                                    Summer Solstice (longest day)

**22** **Thursday**

**23** **Friday**

**24** **Saturday**

**25** **Sunday**

# July 2017

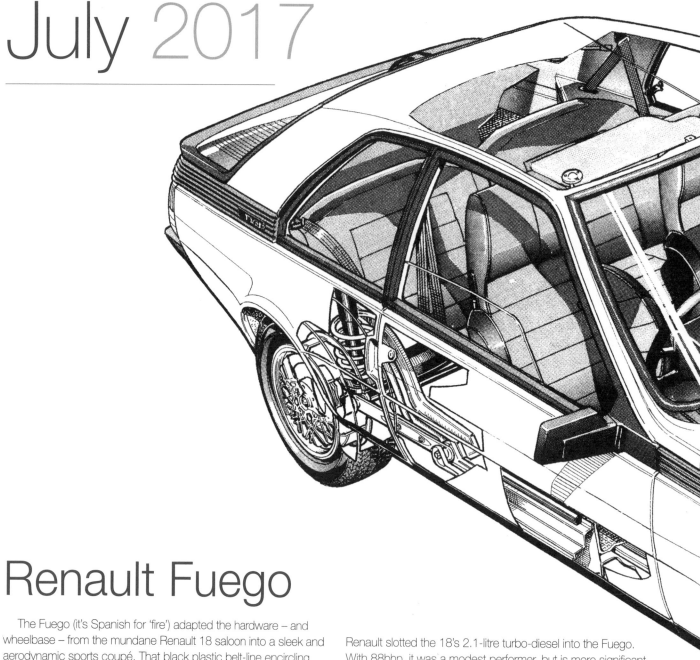

# Renault Fuego

The Fuego (it's Spanish for 'fire') adapted the hardware – and wheelbase – from the mundane Renault 18 saloon into a sleek and aerodynamic sports coupé. That black plastic belt-line encircling the bodywork was distinctive, while the panoramic glass hatchback gave ample headroom in the back for two adults.

Engines ranged from an economical, low-hassle 1.4-litre motor developing 64bhp up to a 110bhp 2-litre. But in 1984 Renault also produced the Fuego Turbo, with a blown 1.6-litre engine putting out 132bhp through the front wheels; the torque-steer was almost as obscene as the huge stickers on the doors reading 'TURBO', for the benefit of anyone who hadn't already twigged.

Nor was the turbo the most interesting engine. A year before,

Renault slotted the 18's 2.1-litre turbo-diesel into the Fuego. With 88bhp, it was a modest performer, but is more significant for being the first vaguely sporting car with diesel power.

And the innovations didn't stop there, either. In the electronic spirit of the early 1980s, the Fuego was the first car with a remote central locking system.

In truth, the car was not the committed performance driver's choice. The spongy MacPherson strut suspension, betraying the Renault 18 within, had been devised for comfort rather than agility. However, on smooth, straight roads, the Fuego's stability and ride was excellent, probably thanks also to a low drag factor of just 0.34.

## Month **Planner**

| Saturday | Sunday | Monday | Tuesday | Wednesday | Thursday | Friday | Saturday | Sunday | Monday | Tuesday | Wednesday | Thursday | Friday | Saturday | Sunday |
|---|---|---|---|---|---|---|---|---|---|---|---|---|---|---|---|
| 1 | 2 | 3 | 4 | 5 | 6 | 7 | 8 | 9 | 10 | 11 | 12 | 13 | 14 | 15 | 16 |

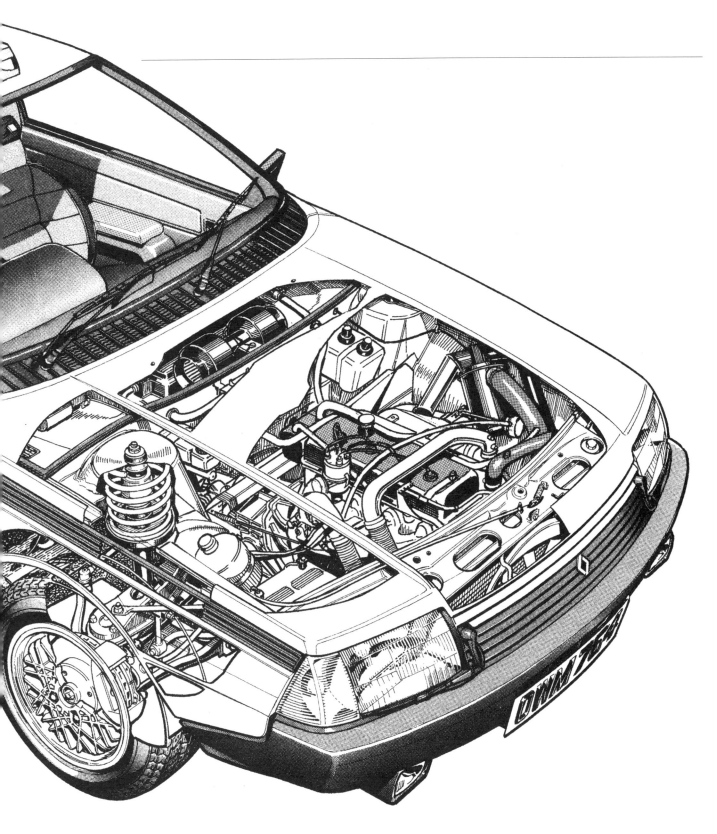

| Monday | Tuesday | Wednesday | Thursday | Friday | Saturday | Sunday | Monday | Tuesday | Wednesday | Thursday | Friday | Saturday | Sunday | Monday |
|---|---|---|---|---|---|---|---|---|---|---|---|---|---|---|
| 17 | 18 | 19 | 20 | 21 | 22 | 23 | 24 | 25 | 26 | 27 | 28 | 29 | 30 | 31 |

**26** **Monday**

**27** **Tuesday**

**28** **Wednesday**

**29** **Thursday**

**30** **Friday**

**1** **Saturday**

**2** **Sunday**

JUN

JUL

3 **Monday**

4 **Tuesday**

5 **Wednesday**

6 **Thursday**

7 **Friday**

8 **Saturday**

9 **Sunday**

**10** **Monday**

**11** **Tuesday**

**12** **Wednesday**                    Holiday (Battle of the Boyne) (NI only)

JUL

## 13 Thursday

## 14 Friday

## 15 Saturday

## 16 Sunday

JUL

**17** **Monday**

JUL

**18** **Tuesday**

**19** **Wednesday**

## 20 Thursday

## 21 Friday

## 22 Saturday

## 23 Sunday

**24** **Monday**

**25** **Tuesday**

JUL

**26** **Wednesday**

## 27 **Thursday**

## 28 **Friday**

JUL

## 29 **Saturday**

## 30 **Sunday**

# August 2017

**AM GENERAL HUMVEE**
1985 onwards (all military variants)
**Enthusiasts' Manual**
An insight into owning, restoring, servicing and driving the US Army's iconic high-mobility multi-purpose wheeled vehicle (HMMWV)

Haynes

## Month **Planner**

| Tuesday | Wednesday | Thursday | Friday | Saturday | Sunday | Monday | Tuesday | Wednesday | Thursday | Friday | Saturday | Sunday | Monday | Tuesday | Wednesday |
|---|---|---|---|---|---|---|---|---|---|---|---|---|---|---|---|
| 1 | 2 | 3 | 4 | 5 | 6 | 7 | 8 | 9 | 10 | 11 | 12 | 13 | 14 | 15 | 16 |

JOHN LAWSON

# Humvee

In the 30 years since it first appeared, the Humvee has become one of the world's most recognisable military vehicles. This versatile and extremely capable machine has accompanied the US Army on operations in Afghanistan, Africa, the Middle East, and the former Yugoslavia. In addition, Humvees are in service with more than 50 other nations.

Development of what was described as the 'high-mobility multi-purpose wheeled vehicle' (HMMWV) started in 1979. AM General was one of just three companies that submitted production proposals, and was awarded a manufacturing contract in March 1983. The first example of what became known as the Humvee rolled off the production line in January 1984, forming part of an initial range of 16 variants. The powerful V8 engine and innovative driveline provided an extraordinary level of off-road performance, combined with the ability to reach high speeds on hard surfaces.

Although never envisaged as an armoured fighting vehicle, there were factory variants described as having either 'basic armour' or 'supplemental armour', but, when faced with the roadside bombs that were commonplace in Iraq and Afghanistan, the Humvee's shortcomings became apparent. So began a cycle of up-armouring. More armour meant more weight, and more weight put additional strain on the chassis and drivetrain, which eventually sounded the death knell for the vehicle. In 2011, the US government announced that the Humvee would be replaced by the all-new joint light tactical vehicle (JLTV). Humvee production, at least for the US Army, ended with more than 281,000 examples constructed.

| Thursday | Friday | Saturday | Sunday | Monday | Tuesday | Wednesday | Thursday | Friday | Saturday | Sunday | Monday | Tuesday | Wednesday | Thursday |
|---|---|---|---|---|---|---|---|---|---|---|---|---|---|---|
| 17 | 18 | 19 | 20 | 21 | 22 | 23 | 24 | 25 | 26 | 27 | 28 | 29 | 30 | 31 |

31 **Monday**

1 **Tuesday**

2 **Wednesday**

3 **Thursday**

4 **Friday**

5 **Saturday**

6 **Sunday**

**7** **Monday**                                    Summer Bank Holiday (Scotland)

**8** **Tuesday**

**9** **Wednesday**

**10** **Thursday**

**11** **Friday**

**12** **Saturday**

**13** **Sunday**

14 **Monday**

15 **Tuesday**

16 **Wednesday**

**17** **Thursday**

**18** **Friday**

**19** **Saturday**

**20** **Sunday**

**21** **Monday**

**22** **Tuesday**

**23** **Wednesday**

**24** **Thursday**

**25** **Friday**

**26** **Saturday**

**27** **Sunday**

AUG

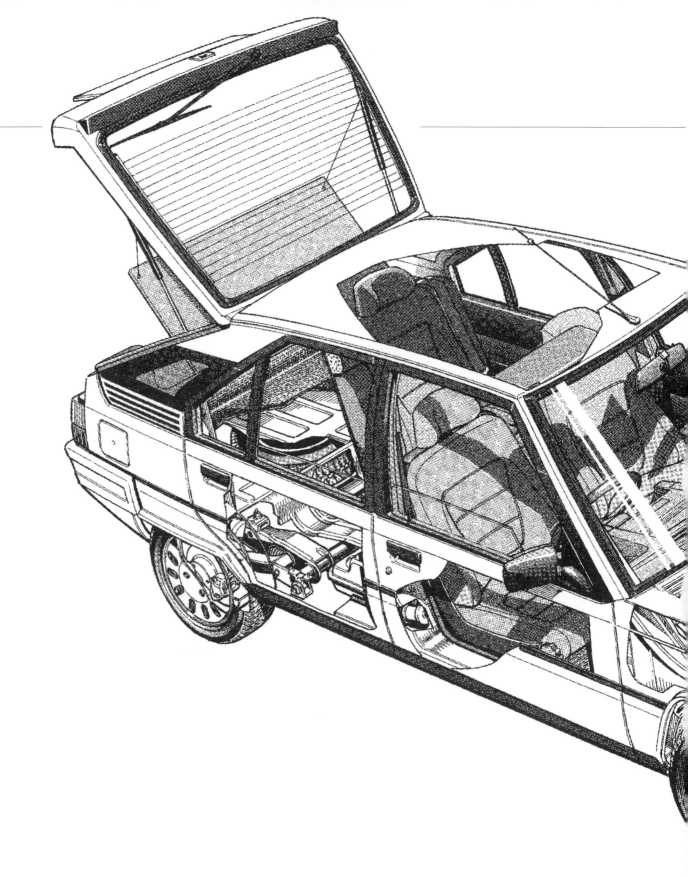

## Month **Planner**

| Friday | Saturday | Sunday | Monday | Tuesday | Wednesday | Thursday | Friday | Saturday | Sunday | Monday | Tuesday | Wednesday | Thursday | Friday | Saturday |
|--------|----------|--------|--------|---------|-----------|----------|--------|----------|--------|--------|---------|-----------|----------|--------|----------|
| 1 | 2 | 3 | 4 | 5 | 6 | 7 | 8 | 9 | 10 | 11 | 12 | 13 | 14 | 15 | 16 |

# Citroen BX

Citroën's history is peppered with landmark models like the Traction Avant, 2CV and DS but, although often overlooked these days, the BX is also a very significant model. It took the best of the eccentricities for which the French company had become renowned – some might say notorious – and packaged them into a 'normal' family car offering space and performance that could equal and better anything from Ford or Volkswagen.

The BX had an all-new platform that incorporated hydropneumatic suspension and powered disc brakes; marque traditionalists might also have approved of the single-spoke steering wheel and controls in dash-mounted drums rather than on stalks.

Indeed, this was the first corporate model developed by the Peugeot group which made its debut as a Citroën; the Bertone-styled BX formed the basis of the Pininfarina-penned Peugeot 405 five years later. So, of course, it featured Peugeot 1.3- and 1.6-litre engines from the start, while for certain markets there was a gutless if thrifty 1.1. Beginning in 1984, the company's excellent diesel and later turbodiesel units were offered, while the GTi could boast France's first-ever 16-valve engine.

There were some other innovations, too. The BX was among the first family saloons to offer the option of four-wheel drive, while the car broke new ground in its use of weight-saving plastic, having a glass fibre bonnet, hatchback and bumpers.

| Sunday | Monday | Tuesday | Wednesday | Thursday | Friday | Saturday | Sunday | Monday | Tuesday | Wednesday | Thursday | Friday | Saturday |
|--------|--------|---------|-----------|----------|--------|----------|--------|--------|---------|-----------|----------|--------|----------|
| 17 | 18 | 19 | 20 | 21 | 22 | 23 | 24 | 25 | 26 | 27 | 28 | 29 | 30 |

**28** **Monday**                                    Summer Bank Holiday (not Scotland)

**29** **Tuesday**

**30** **Wednesday**

**31** **Thursday**

**1** **Friday**

**2** **Saturday**

**3** **Sunday**

4 **Monday**

5 **Tuesday**

6 **Wednesday**

7 **Thursday**

8 **Friday**

9 **Saturday**

10 **Sunday**

11 **Monday**

12 **Tuesday**

13 **Wednesday**

**14** **Thursday**

**15** **Friday**

**16** **Saturday**

**17** **Sunday**

**18** **Monday**

**19** **Tuesday**

**20** **Wednesday**

**21** **Thursday**

**22** **Friday**                                                                                      Autumn Equinox

**23** **Saturday**

**24** **Sunday**

# October 2017

## Honda C90

Honda's ubiquitous Super Cub has provided transport for millions of riders, commuters of all ages, delivery bikes, even taxis in some countries. It's been the chosen ride for a few quirky long-distance adventurers and display teams, and attracted celebrities for various biking challenges.

Starting with the C100 model of 1958, the range has been produced with 50, 70, 90 and 110 cc engines. The C90 has been the most popular in the UK and remained in production much longer than the others. Although the Cub has been updated over the years, important features of its original design have been retained, such as the full legshield, enclosed rear chain, 17-inch spoked wheels and clutchless semi-automatic transmission. The distinctive horizontal engine has been upgraded from overhead valve to overhead cam, the coil and contact breaker ignition replaced by CDI, and the electrics uprated from 6V to 12V. In all this time there had been no practical need to move away from its wire spoked wheels, drum brakes or leading link front suspension and to have done so would have lost some of the little bike's charm. Production of Honda's Super Cub passed the 87 million mark in 2014.

Although now discontinued in Europe due to stringent emission laws, the Honda Super Cub lives on in other world markets. Licencing of the product has enabled Chinese manufacturers to build the Cub for their home market and export, so it is still possible to see modern day examples of the bike albeit incorporating a disc front brake, cast wheels and conventional telescopic forks.

## Month **Planner**

| Sunday | Monday | Tuesday | Wednesday | Thursday | Friday | Saturday | Sunday | Monday | Tuesday | Wednesday | Thursday | Friday | Saturday | Sunday | Monday |
|---|---|---|---|---|---|---|---|---|---|---|---|---|---|---|---|
| 1 | 2 | 3 | 4 | 5 | 6 | 7 | 8 | 9 | 10 | 11 | 12 | 13 | 14 | 15 | 16 |

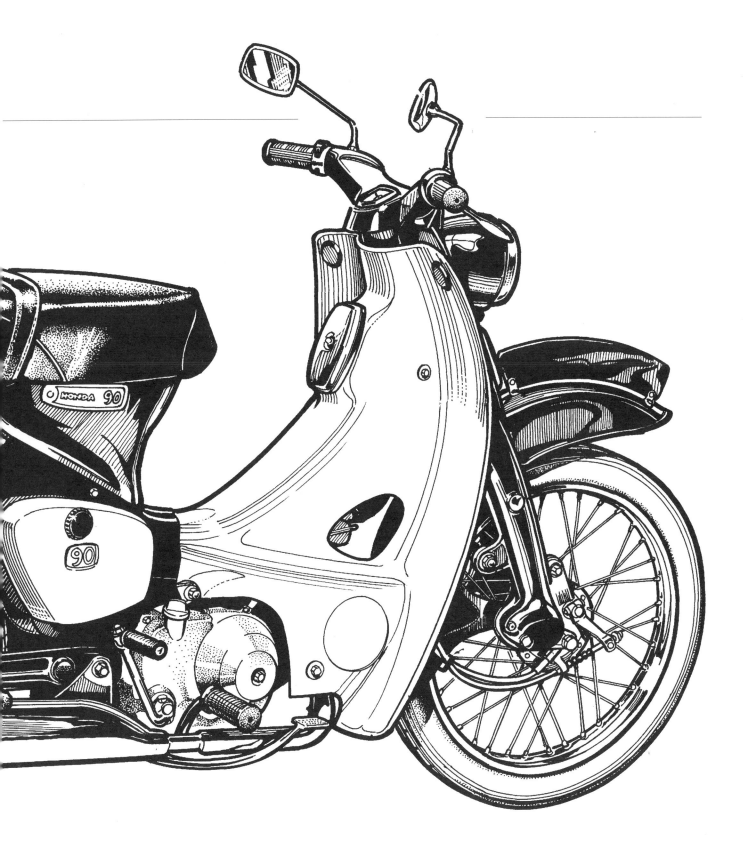

| Tuesday | Wednesday | Thursday | Friday | Saturday | Sunday | Monday | Tuesday | Wednesday | Thursday | Friday | Saturday | Sunday | Monday | Tuesday |
|---------|-----------|----------|--------|----------|--------|--------|---------|-----------|----------|--------|----------|--------|--------|---------|
| 17 | 18 | 19 | 20 | 21 | 22 | 23 | 24 | 25 | 26 | 27 | 28 | 29 | 30 | 31 |

**25** **Monday**

**26** **Tuesday**

**27** **Wednesday**

**28** **Thursday**

**29** **Friday**

**30** **Saturday**

**1** **Sunday**

## 2 Monday

## 3 Tuesday

## 4 Wednesday

**5** **Thursday**

**6** **Friday**

**7** **Saturday**

**8** **Sunday**

**9** **Monday**

**10** **Tuesday**

**11** **Wednesday**

**12** **Thursday**

**13** **Friday**

**14** **Saturday**

**15** **Sunday**

**16** **Monday**

**17** **Tuesday**

**18** **Wednesday**

**19** **Thursday**

**20** **Friday**

**21** **Saturday**

**22** **Sunday**

OCT

**23** **Monday**

**24** **Tuesday**

**25** **Wednesday**

## 26 **Thursday**

## 27 **Friday**

## 28 **Saturday**

## 29 **Sunday**

British Summer Time ends

# Austin Montego

The Montego was the conventional four-door saloon alternative to the Maestro, the car being developed from the same British Leyland-instigated platform. While the Maestro had been known as the LC10 or LM10 during its development phase, the Montego was codenamed LM11. The cars had

actually been on the drawing board since 1975, but only got the go-ahead after protracted negotiations with the British government, Prime Minister Margaret Thatcher being notably reluctant to bankroll the project.

As it turned out, the Montego was well received, with only a few teething problems at the start of production. For once, it was exactly the right size to compete with the Vauxhall Cavalier in the all-important fleet market, and probably benefited from

shifting sentiments among Ford Cortina owners and users who didn't like the new Sierra.

Innovations on the Montego were few, although the body-colour bumpers and windscreen wipers that parked out of sight were neat touches. Obviously, the entire front and rear sections were markedly different to the Maestro. The Montego estate was a notably handsome load-carrier that put a BL-sourced car back on many gravel drives in moneyed suburbia, but the MG Montego Turbo proved an unruly handful with its 150-plus brake-horsepower scrabbling for traction through the front wheels. Like the Maestro, all Montegos bar the MGs were sold as Rovers rather than Austins from 1987.

## Month **Planner**

| Wednesday | Thursday | Friday | Saturday | Sunday | Monday | Tuesday | Wednesday | Thursday | Friday | Saturday | Sunday | Monday | Tuesday | Wednesday | Thursday |
|---|---|---|---|---|---|---|---|---|---|---|---|---|---|---|---|
| 1 | 2 | 3 | 4 | 5 | 6 | 7 | 8 | 9 | 10 | 11 | 12 | 13 | 14 | 15 | 16 |

# November 2017

| Friday | Saturday | Sunday | Monday | Tuesday | Wednesday | Thursday | Friday | Saturday | Sunday | Monday | Tuesday | Wednesda | Thursday |
|---|---|---|---|---|---|---|---|---|---|---|---|---|---|
| 17 | 18 | 19 | 20 | 21 | 22 | 23 | 24 | 25 | 26 | 27 | 28 | 29 | 30 |

**30** **Monday**

**31** **Tuesday**                                                    Hallowe'en

**1** **Wednesday**

**2** **Thursday**

**3** **Friday**

**4** **Saturday**

**5** **Sunday**

6 **Monday**

7 **Tuesday**

8 **Wednesday**

**9** **Thursday**

**10** **Friday**

**11** **Saturday**

**12** **Sunday**                                          Remembrance Sunday

**13** **Monday**

**14** **Tuesday**

**15** **Wednesday**

**16** **Thursday**

**17** **Friday**

**18** **Saturday**

**19** **Sunday**

**20** **Monday**

**21** Tuesday

**22** Wednesday

**23** **Thursday**

**24** **Friday**

**25** **Saturday**

**26** **Sunday**

NOV

# December 2017

## HMS *Alliance*

Launched in 1945 and commissioned two years later, submarine HMS *Alliance* was built by Vickers-Armstrong at Barrow-in-Furness for service with the Royal Navy in the Far East. Planned as part of the 1943 Emergency Building Programme, the Amphion-class (or 'A' class) diesel-electric submarines were capable of high surface speed. They had the capacity and endurance to undertake long-range patrols and they could dive deeper than the previous S- and T-class boats. Initially armed with 10 torpedo tubes, a 4-inch deck gun and a 20mm Oerlikon cannon, they were among the most formidably armed submarines of the time. *Alliance* enjoyed a long and distinguished career spanning more than 28 years that took her all over the world. Today, fully restored, she is the centrepiece at the Royal Navy Submarine Museum, Gosport, where the submarine experience is brought to life by tours around the boat.

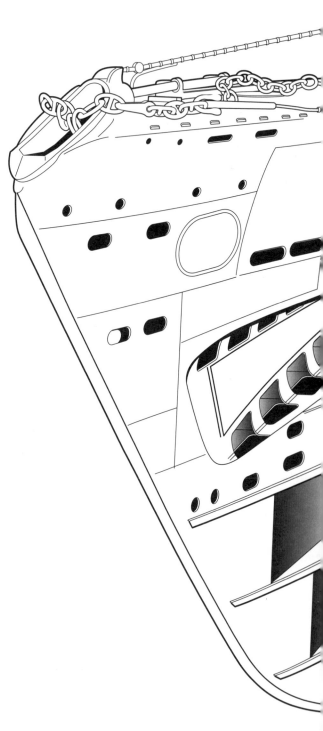

## Month **Planner**

| Friday | Saturday | Sunday | Monday | Tuesday | Wednesday | Thursday | Friday | Saturday | Sunday | Monday | Tuesday | Wednesday | Thursday | Friday | Saturday |
|--------|----------|--------|--------|---------|-----------|----------|--------|----------|--------|--------|---------|-----------|----------|--------|----------|
| 1 | 2 | 3 | 4 | 5 | 6 | 7 | 8 | 9 | 10 | 11 | 12 | 13 | 14 | 15 | 16 |

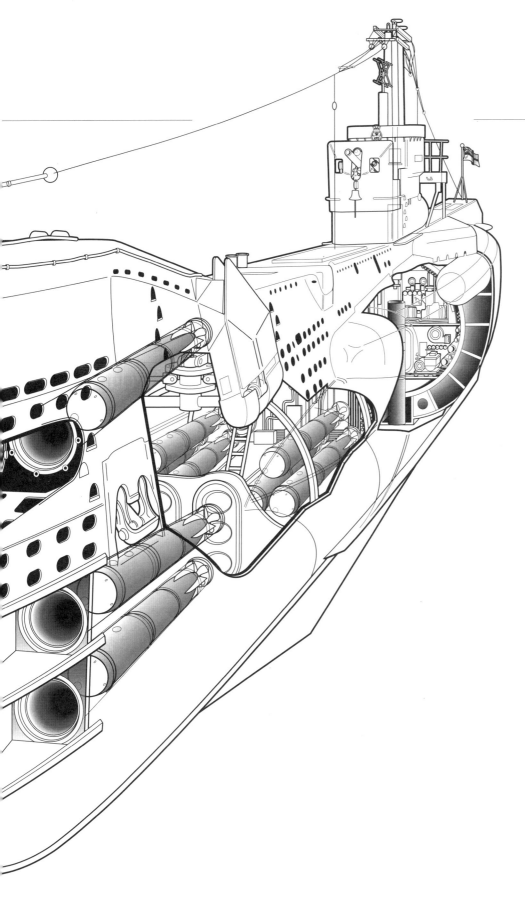

| Sunday | Monday | Tuesday | Wednesday | Thursday | Friday | Saturday | Sunday | Monday | Tuesday | Wednesday | Thursday | Friday | Saturday | Sunday |
|--------|--------|---------|-----------|----------|--------|----------|--------|--------|---------|-----------|----------|--------|----------|--------|
| 17 | 18 | 19 | 20 | 21 | 22 | 23 | 24 | 25 | 26 | 27 | 28 | 29 | 30 | 31 |

27 **Monday**

28 **Tuesday**

29 **Wednesday**

**30** **Thursday**                                   St Andrew's Day (Scotland)

**1** **Friday**

**2** **Saturday**

**3** **Sunday**

4 **Monday**

5 **Tuesday**

6 **Wednesday**

## 7 Thursday

## 8 Friday

## 9 Saturday

## 10 Sunday

11 **Monday**

12 **Tuesday**

13 **Wednesday**

**14** **Thursday**

**15** **Friday**

**16** **Saturday**

**17** **Sunday**

**18** **Monday**

**19** **Tuesday**

**20** **Wednesday**

**21** **Thursday**                                          Winter Solstice (shortest day)

**22** **Friday**

**23** **Saturday**

**24** **Sunday**                                          Christmas Eve

**25** **Monday**                                                    Christmas Day

**26** **Tuesday**                                        Boxing Day (Bank Holiday)

**27** **Wednesday**

**28** **Thursday**

**29** **Friday**

**30** **Saturday**

**31** **Sunday**                                                    New Year's Eve

**1** **Monday**

New Year's Day

**2** **Tuesday**

**3** **Wednesday**

**4** **Thursday**

**5** **Friday**

**6** **Saturday**

**7** **Sunday**

# Appointments **January 2018**

| | |
|---|---|
| Monday 1 | Wednesday 17 |
| Tuesday 2 | Thursday 18 |
| Wednesday 3 | Friday 19 |
| Thursday 4 | Saturday 20 |
| Friday 5 | **Sunday 21** |
| Saturday 6 | Monday 22 |
| **Sunday 7** | Tuesday 23 |
| Monday 8 | Wednesday 24 |
| Tuesday 9 | Thursday 25 |
| Wednesday 10 | Friday 26 |
| Thursday 11 | Saturday 27 |
| Friday 12 | **Sunday 28** |
| Saturday 13 | Monday 29 |
| **Sunday 14** | Tuesday 30 |
| Monday 15 | Wedesday 31 |
| Tuesday 16 | |

# Appointments **February 2018**

Thursday
1

Friday
2

Saturday
3

**Sunday**
**4**

Monday
5

Tuesday
6

Wednesday
7

Thursday
8

Friday
9

Saturday
10

**Sunday**
**11**

Monday
12

Tuesday
13

Wednesday
14

Thursday
15

Friday
16

Saturday
17

**Sunday**
**18**

Monday
19

Tuesday
20

Wednesday
21

Thursday
22

Friday
23

Saturday
24

**Sunday**
**25**

Monday
26

Tuesday
27

Wednesday
28

# Appointments **March 2018**

| | |
|---|---|
| Thursday<br>1 | Saturday<br>17 |
| Friday<br>2 | **Sunday**<br>**18** |
| Saturday<br>3 | Monday<br>19 |
| **Sunday**<br>**4** | Tuesday<br>20 |
| Monday<br>5 | Wednesday<br>21 |
| Tuesday<br>6 | Thursday<br>22 |
| Wednesday<br>7 | Friday<br>23 |
| Thursday<br>8 | Saturday<br>24 |
| Friday<br>9 | **Sunday**<br>**25** |
| Saturday<br>10 | Monday<br>26 |
| **Sunday**<br>**11** | Tuesday<br>27 |
| Monday<br>12 | Wednesday<br>28 |
| Tuesday<br>13 | Thursday<br>29 |
| Wednesday<br>14 | Friday<br>30 |
| Thursday<br>15 | Saturday<br>31 |
| Friday<br>16 | |

# Appointments **April 2018**

| | |
|---|---|
| **Sunday** **1** | Tuesday 17 |
| Monday 2 | Wednesday 18 |
| Tuesday 3 | Thursday 19 |
| Wednesday 4 | Friday 20 |
| Thursday 5 | Saturday 21 |
| Friday 6 | **Sunday** **22** |
| Saturday 7 | Monday 23 |
| **Sunday** **8** | Tuesday 24 |
| Monday 9 | Wednesday 25 |
| Tuesday 10 | Thursday 26 |
| Wednesday 11 | Friday 27 |
| Thursday 12 | Saturday 28 |
| Friday 13 | **Sunday** **29** |
| Saturday 14 | Monday 30 |
| **Sunday** **15** | |
| Monday 16 | |

# Appointments **May 2018**

| | |
|---|---|
| Tuesday<br>1 | Thursday<br>17 |
| Wednesday<br>2 | Friday<br>18 |
| Thursday<br>3 | Saturday<br>19 |
| Friday<br>4 | **Sunday**<br>**20** |
| Saturday<br>5 | Monday<br>21 |
| **Sunday**<br>**6** | Tuesday<br>22 |
| Monday<br>7 | Wednesday<br>23 |
| Tuesday<br>8 | Thursday<br>24 |
| Wednesday<br>9 | Friday<br>25 |
| Thursday<br>10 | Saturday<br>26 |
| Friday<br>11 | **Sunday**<br>**27** |
| Saturday<br>12 | Monday<br>28 |
| **Sunday**<br>**13** | Tuesday<br>29 |
| Monday<br>14 | Wednesday<br>30 |
| Tuesday<br>15 | Thursday<br>31 |
| Wednesday<br>16 | |

# Appointments **June 2018**

| | |
|---|---|
| Friday **1** | Sunday **17** |
| Saturday **2** | Monday **18** |
| **Sunday 3** | Tuesday **19** |
| Monday **4** | Wednesday **20** |
| Tuesday **5** | Thursday **21** |
| Wednesday **6** | Friday **22** |
| Thursday **7** | Saturday **23** |
| Friday **8** | **Sunday 24** |
| Saturday **9** | Monday **25** |
| **Sunday 10** | Tuesday **26** |
| Monday **11** | Wednesday **27** |
| Tuesday **12** | Thursday **28** |
| Wednesday **13** | Friday **29** |
| Thursday **14** | Saturday **30** |
| Friday **15** | |
| Saturday **16** | |

# Haynes: the story so far

Haynes Publishing is known the world over for car and motorcycle repair manuals. It is the market leader for practical and authoritative reference works on DIY maintenance and servicing of vehicles, and has gained an enviable reputation in half a century of publishing. Every Haynes manual is based on a complete strip-down and rebuild of a vehicle in the company's workshops, ensuring that instructions and illustrations are accurate, practical and easy to follow.

J H Haynes & Co was formed on 18 May 1960, but the origins of today's publishing success can be traced back even further. In 1954, John Haynes, then aged 16 and still at school, built an Austin Seven Special and was inspired to write and publish a book on how he had done it. This was *Building a 750cc Special,* which went on sale in 1956.

After leaving school, John served in the RAF but still found time to develop his long-term passion of publishing practical motoring books. The first workshop manual was published after he helped a friend restore a 'frog-eye' Austin-Healey Sprite, having found that the manufacturer's own publications were totally inadequate from a DIY point of view.

With help from his father Harold, wife Annette and younger brother David, the business was built up, always following a philosophy of self-sufficiency and direct control over all aspects of publishing. From writing, editing and printing to sales, marketing and distribution, this policy continues to the present day. As the number of employed staff increased and output expanded, various new premises

were required and eventually, in 1972, the site of an old creamery on the A303 at Sparkford, near Yeovil in Somerset, was taken over – this remains the company's headquarters today.

Attention also turned to the USA and a subsidiary was set up in California in 1974. North America has since become the largest market for Haynes with turnover having grown to twice the UK figure. The range of manuals available in North America has more recently been enhanced by the acquisition of former rival Chilton in 2002. Offices and subsidiary companies also operate in Australia, Sweden and The Netherlands.

The continuing success of the original company led to flotation on the London Stock Exchange in 1979 and the launch of the Haynes Publishing Group PLC.

The very beginning. John Haynes with his 1954 Austin Seven Special, taken with a Brownie box camera.

The Haynes project workshop team hard at work on yet another manual, this time for the new Mini.

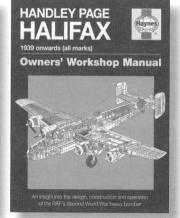

The Haynes family involvement, however, has remained strong ever since. Although he retired as Chairman upon the company's 50th anniversary, John Haynes OBE (he was recognised for his services to publishing in the Queen's 1995 Birthday Honours List) still sits on the Main Board as Founder Director and remains a major shareholder. His oldest son, J, who joined the business in 2002, has taken over as Chief Executive to steer the Group into the next phase of its evolution.

Having established a flourishing book publishing business based on his personal interest in cars and motorcycles, it was logical for John Haynes to build up a collection of vehicles that appealed to him. He started to acquire a few interesting cars in the late 1960s and the collection expanded rapidly, becoming so large that a permanent museum was required to house and maintain them all. The Haynes International Motor Museum, the Charitable Trust to which John donated almost all of his collection, opened in July 1985 and, like the publishing company, subsequently grew out of all recognition. It is now the UK's largest permanent exhibition of cars and motorcycles. It is a living and working museum with more than 350 vehicles in 11 display halls together with extensive workshop facilities to ensure that exhibits are maintained in first-class operational condition.

Nowadays Haynes Publishing is about much more than car manuals. It publishes an extensive range of manuals on motorsport, military, aviation, maritime and railway subjects, as well as manuals in areas such as computing, health, sport and DIY.

A number of other transport publishers – notably G.T. Foulis and Patrick Stephens Limited – have been acquired at different times and absorbed under the Haynes banner.

So it can be seen that Haynes Publishing has come a long way since an Austin Seven was bought as a DIY project for just £15, and when the net profit from the first year of mail-order trading in books, in 1958, was £843 16s 10d. Fifty years on, Haynes Publishing Group's worldwide operating profit has increased almost 1000-fold!

To learn more and to view Haynes' entire range of publications, please visit our website **www.haynes.co.uk**.

Just part of the amazing 'Red Collection' of sports cars on display at the Haynes International Motor Museum.

Annette and John Haynes on the occasion of his OBE presentation.

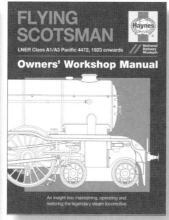

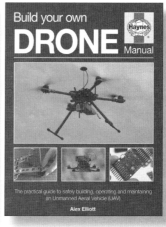

# Conversion Factors

## Length (distance)

| | | | | | | |
|---|---|---|---|---|---|---|
| Inches (in) | x 25.4 | = | Millimetres (mm) | x 0.0394 | = | Inches (in) |
| Feet (ft) | x 0.305 | = | Metres (m) | x 3.281 | = | Feet (ft) |
| Miles | x 1.609 | = | Kilometres (km) | x 0.621 | = | Miles |

## Volume (capacity)

| | | | | | | |
|---|---|---|---|---|---|---|
| Cubic inches (cu in; in$^3$) | x 16.387 | = | Cubic centimetres (cc; cm$^3$) | x 0.061 | = | Cubic inches (cu in; in$^3$) |
| Imperial pints (Imp pt) | x 0.568 | = | Litres (l) | x 1.76 | = | Imperial pints (Imp pt) |
| Imperial quarts (Imp qt) | x 1.137 | = | Litres (l) | x 0.88 | = | Imperial quarts (Imp qt) |
| Imperial quarts (Imp qt) | x 1.201 | = | US quarts (US qt) | x 0.833 | = | Imperial quarts (Imp qt) |
| US quarts (US qt) | x 0.946 | = | Litres (l) | x 1.057 | = | US quarts (US qt) |
| Imperial gallons (Imp gal) | x 4.546 | = | Litres (l) | x 0.22 | = | Imperial gallons (Imp gal) |
| Imperial gallons (Imp gal) | x 1.201 | = | US gallons (US gal) | x 0.833 | = | Imperial gallons (Imp gal) |
| US gallons (US gal) | x 3.785 | = | Litres (l) | x 0.264 | = | US gallons (US gal) |

## Mass (weight)

| | | | | | | |
|---|---|---|---|---|---|---|
| Ounces (oz) | x 28.35 | = | Grams (g) | x 0.035 | = | Ounces (oz) |
| Pounds (lb) | x 0.454 | = | Kilograms (kg) | x 2.205 | = | Pounds (lb) |

## Force

| | | | | | | |
|---|---|---|---|---|---|---|
| Ounces-force (ozf; oz) | x 0.278 | = | Newtons (N) | x 3.6 | = | Ounces-force (ozf; oz) |
| Pounds-force (lbf; lb) | x 4.448 | = | Newtons (N) | x 0.225 | = | Pounds-force (lbf; lb) |
| Newtons (N) | x 0.1 | = | Kilograms-force (kgf; kg) | x 9.81 | = | Newtons (N) |

## Pressure

| | | | | | | |
|---|---|---|---|---|---|---|
| Pounds-force per square inch (psi; lbf/in$^2$; lb/in$^2$) | x 0.070 | = | Kilograms-force per square centimetre (kgf/cm$^2$; kg/cm$^2$) | x 14.223 | = | Pounds-force per square inch (psi; lbf/in$^2$; lb/in$^2$) |
| Pounds-force per square inch (psi; lbf/in$^2$; lb/in$^2$) | x 0.068 | = | Atmospheres (atm) | x 14.696 | = | Pounds-force per square inch (psi; lbf/in$^2$; lb/in$^2$) |
| Pounds-force per square inch (psi; lbf/in$^2$; lb/in$^2$) | x 0.069 | = | Bars | x 14.5 | = | Pounds-force per square inch (psi; lbf/in$^2$; lb/in$^2$) |
| Pounds-force per square inch (psi; lbf/in$^2$; lb/in$^2$) | x 6.895 | = | Kilopascals (kPa) | x 0.145 | = | Pounds-force per square inch (psi; lbf/in$^2$; lb/in$^2$) |
| Kilopascals (kPa) | x 0.01 | = | Kilograms-force per square centimetre (kgf/cm$^2$; kg/cm$^2$) | x 98.1 | = | Kilopascals (kPa) |
| Millibar (mbar) | x 100 | = | Pascals (Pa) | x 0.01 | = | Millibar (mbar) |
| Millibar (mbar) | x 0.0145 | = | Pounds-force per square inch (psi; lbf/in$^2$; lb/in$^2$) | x 68.947 | = | Millibar (mbar) |
| Millibar (mbar) | x 0.75 | = | Millimetres of mercury (mmHg) | x 1.333 | = | Millibar (mbar) |
| Millibar (mbar) | x 0.401 | = | Inches of water (inH$_2$O) | x 2.491 | = | Millibar (mbar) |
| Millimetres of mercury (mmHg) | x 0.535 | = | Inches of water (inH$_2$O) | x 1.868 | = | Millimetres of mercury (mmHg) |
| Inches of water (inH$_2$O) | x 0.036 | = | Pounds-force per square inch (psi; lbf/in$^2$; lb/in$^2$) | x 27.68 | = | Inches of water (inH$_2$O) |

## Torque (moment of force)

| | | | | | | |
|---|---|---|---|---|---|---|
| Pounds-force inches (lbf in; lb in) | x 1.152 | = | Kilograms-force centimetre (kgf cm; kg cm) | x 0.868 | = | Pounds-force inches (lbf in; lb in) |
| Pounds-force inches (lbf in; lb in) | x 0.113 | = | Newton metres (Nm) | x 8.85 | = | Pounds-force inches (lbf in; lb in) |
| Pounds-force inches (lbf in; lb in) | x 0.083 | = | Pounds-force feet (lbf ft; lb ft) | x 12 | = | Pounds-force inches (lbf in; lb in) |
| Pounds-force feet (lbf ft; lb ft) | x 0.138 | = | Kilograms-force metres (kgf m; kg m) | x 7.233 | = | Pounds-force feet (lbf ft; lb ft) |
| Pounds-force feet (lbf ft; lb ft) | x 1.356 | = | Newton metres (Nm) | x 0.738 | = | Pounds-force feet (lbf ft; lb ft) |
| Newton metres (Nm) | x 0.102 | = | Kilograms-force metres (kgf m; kg m) | x 9.804 | = | Newton metres (Nm) |

## Power

| | | | | | | |
|---|---|---|---|---|---|---|
| Horsepower (hp) | x 745.7 | = | Watts (W) | x 0.0013 | = | Horsepower (hp) |

## Velocity (speed)

| | | | | | | |
|---|---|---|---|---|---|---|
| Miles per hour (miles/hr; mph) | x 1.609 | = | Kilometres per hour (km/hr; kph) | x 0.621 | = | Miles per hour (miles/hr; mph) |

## Fuel consumption*

| | | | | | | |
|---|---|---|---|---|---|---|
| Miles per gallon, Imperial (mpg) | x 0.354 | = | Kilometres per litre (km/l) | x 2.825 | = | Miles per gallon, Imperial (mpg) |
| Miles per gallon, US (mpg) | x 0.425 | = | Kilometres per litre (km/l) | x 2.352 | = | Miles per gallon, US (mpg) |

## Temperature

Degrees Fahrenheit = (°C x 1.8) + 32    Degrees Celsius (Degrees Centigrade; °C) = (°F − 32) x 0.56

*It is common practice to convert from miles per gallon (mpg) to litres/100 kilometres (l/100km), where mpg x l/100 km = 282*

# UK MAINLAND VEHICLE
# REGISTRATION LETTERS

### Registration marks:

From 1st September 2001 registration marks took the form: **AB52 CCC** where **A** is the area identifier, **B** is the vehicle registration office. **52** identifies the year, the first digit is the period, either **0** or **1** (March to August) or **5** or **6** (September to February), the second digit is the year in which the period starts. **CCC** is a random combination of letters.

The registration letter should not be regarded as an infallible indication of vehicle age. **Refer to the registration document for confirmation.**

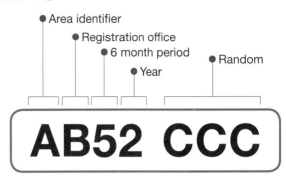

- Area identifier
- Registration office
- 6 month period
- Year
- Random

## AB52 CCC

| SUFFIX | | | | | | |
|---|---|---|---|---|---|---|
| Jan 1 | 1963 | > | Dec 31 | 1963 | | A |
| Jan 1 | 1964 | > | Dec 31 | 1964 | | B |
| Jan 1 | 1965 | > | Dec 31 | 1965 | | C |
| Jan 1 | 1966 | > | Dec 31 | 1966 | | D |
| Jan 1 | 1967 | > | July 31 | 1967 | | E |
| Aug 1 | 1967 | > | July 31 | 1968 | | F |
| Aug 1 | 1968 | > | July 31 | 1969 | | G |
| Aug 1 | 1969 | > | July 31 | 1970 | | H |
| Aug 1 | 1970 | > | July 31 | 1971 | | J |
| Aug 1 | 1971 | > | July 31 | 1972 | | K |
| Aug 1 | 1972 | > | July 31 | 1973 | | L |
| Aug 1 | 1973 | > | July 31 | 1974 | | M |
| Aug 1 | 1974 | > | July 31 | 1975 | | N |
| Aug 1 | 1975 | > | July 31 | 1976 | | P |
| Aug 1 | 1976 | > | July 31 | 1977 | | R |
| Aug 1 | 1977 | > | July 31 | 1978 | | S |
| Aug 1 | 1978 | > | July 31 | 1979 | | T |
| Aug 1 | 1979 | > | July 31 | 1980 | | V |
| Aug 1 | 1980 | > | July 31 | 1981 | | W |
| Aug 1 | 1981 | > | July 31 | 1982 | | X |
| Aug 1 | 1982 | > | July 31 | 1983 | | Y |

| PREFIX | | | | | |
|---|---|---|---|---|---|
| A | Aug 1 | 1983 | > | July 31 | 1984 |
| B | Aug 1 | 1984 | > | July 31 | 1985 |
| C | Aug 1 | 1985 | > | July 31 | 1986 |
| D | Aug 1 | 1986 | > | July 31 | 1987 |
| E | Aug 1 | 1987 | > | July 31 | 1988 |
| F | Aug 1 | 1988 | > | July 31 | 1989 |
| G | Aug 1 | 1989 | > | July 31 | 1990 |
| H | Aug 1 | 1990 | > | July 31 | 1991 |
| J | Aug 1 | 1991 | > | July 31 | 1992 |
| K | Aug 1 | 1992 | > | July 31 | 1993 |
| L | Aug 1 | 1993 | > | July 31 | 1994 |
| M | Aug 1 | 1994 | > | July 31 | 1995 |
| N | Aug 1 | 1995 | > | July 31 | 1996 |
| P | Aug 1 | 1996 | > | July 31 | 1997 |
| R | Aug 1 | 1997 | > | July 31 | 1998 |
| S | Aug 1 | 1998 | > | Jan 31 | 1999 |
| T | Feb 1 | 1999 | > | July 31 | 1999 |
| V | Aug 1 | 1999 | > | Feb 29 | 2000 |
| W | Mar 1 | 2000 | > | Aug 31 | 2000 |
| X | Sept 1 | 2000 | > | Feb 28 | 2001 |
| Y | Mar 1 | 2001 | > | Aug 31 | 2001 |

| CENTRAL | | | | | |
|---|---|---|---|---|---|
| Sept 1 | 2001 | > | Feb 28 | 2002 | 51 |
| Mar 1 | 2002 | > | Aug 31 | 2002 | 02 |
| Sept 1 | 2002 | > | Feb 28 | 2003 | 52 |
| Mar 1 | 2003 | > | Aug 31 | 2003 | 03 |
| Sept 1 | 2003 | > | Feb 29 | 2004 | 53 |
| Mar 1 | 2004 | > | Aug 31 | 2004 | 04 |
| Sept 1 | 2004 | > | Feb 28 | 2005 | 54 |
| Mar 1 | 2005 | > | Aug 31 | 2005 | 05 |
| Sept 1 | 2005 | > | Feb 28 | 2006 | 55 |
| Mar 1 | 2006 | > | Aug 31 | 2006 | 06 |
| Sept 1 | 2006 | > | Feb 28 | 2007 | 56 |
| Mar 1 | 2007 | > | Aug 31 | 2007 | 07 |
| Sept 1 | 2007 | > | Feb 29 | 2008 | 57 |
| Mar 1 | 2008 | > | Aug 31 | 2008 | 08 |
| Sept 1 | 2008 | > | Feb 28 | 2009 | 58 |
| Mar 1 | 2009 | > | Aug 31 | 2009 | 09 |
| Sept 1 | 2009 | > | Feb 28 | 2010 | 59 |
| Mar 1 | 2010 | > | Aug 31 | 2010 | 10 |
| Sept 1 | 2010 | > | Feb 28 | 2011 | 60 |
| Mar 1 | 2011 | > | Aug 31 | 2011 | 11 |
| Sept 1 | 2011 | > | Feb 29 | 2012 | 61 |
| Mar 1 | 2012 | > | Aug 31 | 2012 | 12 |
| Sept 1 | 2012 | > | Feb 28 | 2013 | 62 |
| Mar 1 | 2013 | > | Aug 31 | 2013 | 13 |
| Sept 1 | 2013 | > | Feb 28 | 2014 | 63 |
| Mar 1 | 2014 | > | Aug 31 | 2014 | 14 |
| Sept 1 | 2014 | > | Feb 28 | 2015 | 64 |
| Mar 1 | 2015 | > | Aug 31 | 2015 | 15 |
| Sept 1 | 2015 | > | Feb 29 | 2016 | 65 |
| Mar 1 | 2016 | > | Aug 31 | 2016 | 16 |
| Sept 1 | 2016 | > | Feb 29 | 2017 | 66 |
| Mar 1 | 2017 | > | Aug 31 | 2017 | 17 |
| Sept 1 | 2017 | > | Feb 28 | 2018 | 67 |

On the next four pages you will find a complete list of **registration area identification letters** covering the three periods: **pre 1974**, **1974 to 2001** and **September 2001 onwards**.

# UK Number Plate Registration Area Identification Letters

| | Pre 1974 | 1974 to 2001 | September 2001 onwards |
|---|---|---|---|
| A | London | – | |
| AA | Hampshire | Bournemouth | Peterborough |
| AB | Worcestershire | Worcester | Peterborough |
| AC | Warwickshire | Coventry | Peterborough |
| AD | Gloucestershire | Gloucester | Peterborough |
| AE | Bristol | Bristol | Peterborough |
| AF | Cornwall | Truro | Peterborough |
| AG | Ayrshire | Kingston-upon-Hull | Peterborough |
| AH | Norfolk | Norwich | Peterborough |
| AI | Meath | – | – |
| AJ | North Yorkshire | Middlesbrough | Peterborough |
| AK | Bradford | Sheffield | Peterborough |
| AL | Nottinghamshire | Nottingham | Peterborough |
| AM | Wiltshire | Swindon | Peterborough |
| AN | West Ham | Reading | Peterborough |
| AO | Cumberland | Carlisle | Norwich |
| AP | East Sussex | Brighton | Norwich |
| AR | Hertfordshire | Chelmsford | Norwich |
| AS | Nairn | Inverness | Norwich |
| AT | Kingston-upon-Hull | Kingston-upon-Hull | Norwich |
| AU | Nottingham | Nottingham | Norwich |
| AV | Aberdeenshire | Peterborough | Ipswich |
| AW | Shropshire | Shrewsbury | Ipswich |
| AX | Monmouthshire | Cardiff | Ipswich |
| AY | Leicestershire | Leicester | Ipswich |
| AY | Alderney | Alderney | Ipswich |
| AZ | Belfast | Belfast | – |
| B | Lancashire | – | – |
| BA | Salford | Manchester | Birmingham |
| BB | Newcastle-upon-Tyne | Newcastle-upon-Tyne | Birmingham |
| BC | Leicester | Leicester | Birmingham |
| BD | Northamptonshire | Northampton | Birmingham |
| BE | Lincolnshire | Lincoln | Birmingham |
| BF | Staffordshire | Stoke-on-Trent | Birmingham |
| BG | Birkenhead | Liverpool | Birmingham |
| BH | Buckinghamshire | Luton | Birmingham |
| BI | Monaghan | – | Birmingham |
| BJ | East Suffolk | Ipswich | Birmingham |
| BK | Portsmouth | Portsmouth | Birmingham |
| BL | Berkshire | Reading | Birmingham |
| BM | Bedfordshire | Luton | Birmingham |
| BN | Bolton | Manchester | Birmingham |
| BO | Cardiff | Cardiff | Birmingham |
| BP | West Sussex | Portsmouth | Birmingham |
| BR | Sunderland | Newcastle-upon-Tyne | Birmingham |
| BS | Orkney | Aberdeen | Birmingham |
| BT | East Yorkshire | Leeds | Birmingham |
| BU | Oldham | Manchester | Birmingham |
| BV | Blackburn | Preston | Birmingham |
| BW | Oxfordshire | Oxford | Birmingham |
| BX | Carmarthenshire | Haverfordwest | Birmingham |
| BY | Croydon | North West London | Birmingham |
| BZ | Down | Belfast | – |
| C | West Yorkshire | – | – |
| CA | Denbighshire | Chester | Cardiff |
| CB | Blackburn | Manchester | Cardiff |
| CC | Caernarvonshire | Bangor | Cardiff |
| CD | Brighton | Brighton | Cardiff |
| CE | Cambridgeshire | Peterborough | Cardiff |
| CF | West Suffolk | Reading | Cardiff |
| CG | Hampshire | Bournemouth | Cardiff |
| CH | Derby | Nottingham | Cardiff |
| CI | Laois | – | – |
| CJ | Herefordshire | Gloucester | Cardiff |
| CK | Preston | Preston | Cardiff |
| CL | Norwich | Norwich | Cardiff |
| CM | Birkenhead | Liverpool | Cardiff |
| CN | Gateshead | Newcastle-upon-Tyne | Cardiff |
| CO | Plymouth | Exeter | Cardiff |
| CP | Halifax | Huddersfield | Swansea |
| CR | Southampton | Portsmouth | Swansea |
| CS | Ayrshire | Glasgow | Swansea |
| CT | Lincolnshire | Lincoln | Swansea |
| CU | South Shields | Newcastle-upon-Tyne | Swansea |
| CV | Cornwall | Truro | Swansea |
| CW | Burnley | Preston | Bangor |
| CX | Huddersfield | Huddersfield | Bangor |
| CY | Swansea | Swansea | Bangor |
| CZ | Belfast | – | – |

| | Pre 1974 | 1974 to 2001 | September 2001 onwards |
|---|---|---|---|
| D | Kent | – | |
| DA | Wolverhampton | Birmingham | Chester |
| DB | Stockport | Manchester | Chester |
| DC | Middlesbrough | Middlesbrough | Chester |
| DD | Gloucestershire | Gloucester | Chester |
| DE | Pembrokeshire | Haverfordwest | Chester |
| DF | Gloucestershire | Gloucester | Chester |
| DG | Gloucestershire | Gloucester | Chester |
| DH | Walsall | Dudley | Chester |
| DI | Roscommon | – | – |
| DJ | St Helens | Liverpool | Chester |
| DK | Rochdale | Manchester | Chester |
| DL | Isle of Wight | Portsmouth | Shrewsbury |
| DM | Flintshire | Chester | Shrewsbury |
| DN | York | Leeds | Shrewsbury |
| DO | Lincolnshire | Lincoln | Shrewsbury |
| DP | Reading | Reading | Shrewsbury |
| DR | Plymouth | Exeter | Shrewsbury |
| DS | Peeblesshire | Glasgow | Shrewsbury |
| DT | Doncaster | Sheffield | Shrewsbury |
| DU | Coventry | Coventry | Shrewsbury |
| DV | Devon | Exeter | Shrewsbury |
| DW | Newport | Cardiff | Shrewsbury |
| DX | Ipswich | Ipswich | Shrewsbury |
| DY | Hastings | Brighton | Shrewsbury |
| DZ | Antrim | Belfast | – |
| E | Staffordshire | – | – |
| EA | West Bromwich | Dudley | Chelmsford |
| EB | Isle of Ely | Peterborough | Chelmsford |
| EC | Westmorland | Preston | Chelmsford |
| ED | Warrington | Liverpool | Chelmsford |
| EE | Grimsby | Lincoln | Chelmsford |
| EF | West Hartlepool | Middlesbrough | Chelmsford |
| EG | Peterborough | Peterborough | Chelmsford |
| EH | Stoke on Trent | Stoke on Trent | Chelmsford |
| EI | Sligo | – | – |
| EJ | Cardigan | Haverfordwest | Chelmsford |
| EK | Wigan | Liverpool | Chelmsford |
| EL | Bournemouth | Bournemouth | Chelmsford |
| EM | Bootle | Liverpool | Chelmsford |
| EN | Bury | Manchester | Chelmsford |
| EO | Barrow-in-Furness | Preston | Chelmsford |
| EP | Montgomery | Swansea | Chelmsford |
| ER | Cambridgeshire | Peterborough | Chelmsford |
| ES | Perthshire | Dundee | Chelmsford |
| ET | Rotherham | Sheffield | Chelmsford |
| EU | Brecknockshire | Bristol | Chelmsford |
| EV | Essex | Chelmsford | Chelmsford |
| EW | Huntingdon | Peterborough | Chelmsford |
| EX | Great Yarmouth | Norwich | Chelmsford |
| EY | Anglesey | Bangor | Chelmsford |
| EZ | Belfast | – | – |
| FA | Burton-on-Trent | Stoke-on-Trent | Nottingham |
| FB | Bath | Bristol | Nottingham |
| FC | Oxford | Oxford | Nottingham |
| FD | Dudley | Dudley | Nottingham |
| FE | Lincoln | Lincoln | Nottingham |
| FF | Merioneth | Bangor | Nottingham |
| FG | Fife | Brighton | Nottingham |
| FH | Gloucester | Gloucester | Nottingham |
| FI | Tipperary | – | – |
| FJ | Exeter | Exeter | Nottingham |
| FK | Worcester | Dudley | Nottingham |
| FL | Peterborough | Peterborough | Nottingham |
| FM | Chester | Chester | Nottingham |
| FN | Canterbury | Maidstone | Nottingham |
| FO | Radnorshire | Gloucester | Nottingham |
| FP | Rutland | Leicester | Nottingham |
| FR | Blackpool | Preston | Lincoln |
| FS | Edinburgh | Edinburgh | Lincoln |
| FT | Tynemouth | Newcastle-upon-Tyne | Lincoln |
| FU | Lincolnshire | Lincoln | Lincoln |
| FV | Blackpool | Preston | Lincoln |
| FW | Lincolnshire | Lincoln | Lincoln |
| FX | Dorset | Bournemouth | Lincoln |
| FY | Southport | Liverpool | Lincoln |
| FZ | Belfast | – | – |
| G | Glasgow | – | – |
| GA | Glasgow | Glasgow | Maidstone |

| | Pre 1974 | 1974 to 2001 | September 2001 onwards |
|---|---|---|---|
| GB | Glasgow | Glasgow | Maidstone |
| GC | London | South West London | Maidstone |
| GD | Glasgow | Glasgow | Maidstone |
| GE | Glasgow | Glasgow | Maidstone |
| GF | London | South West London | Maidstone |
| GG | Glasgow | Glasgow | Maidstone |
| GH | London | South West London | Maidstone |
| GJ | London | South West London | Maidstone |
| GK | London | South West London | Maidstone |
| GL | Bath | Truro | Maidstone |
| GM | Motherwell | Reading | Maidstone |
| GN | London | South West London | Maidstone |
| GO | London | South West London | Maidstone |
| GP | London | South West London | Brighton |
| GR | Sunderland | Newcastle-upon-Tyne | Brighton |
| GS | Perthshire | Luton | Brighton |
| GT | London | South West London | Brighton |
| GU | London | South East London | Brighton |
| GV | West Suffolk | Ipswich | Brighton |
| GW | London | South East London | Brighton |
| GX | London | South East London | Brighton |
| GY | London | South East London | Brighton |
| GZ | Belfast | – | – |
| H | Middlesex | – | – |
| HA | Smethwick | Dudley | Bournemouth |
| HB | Merthyr Tydfil | Cardiff | Bournemouth |
| HC | Eastbourne | Brighton | Bournemouth |
| HD | Dewsbury | Huddersfield | Bournemouth |
| HE | Barnsley | Sheffield | Bournemouth |
| HF | Wallasey | Liverpool | Bournemouth |
| HG | Burnley | Preston | Bournemouth |
| HH | Carlisle | Carlisle | Bournemouth |
| HI | Tipperary | – | – |
| HJ | Southend | Chelmsford | Bournemouth |
| HK | Essex | Chelmsford | Portsmouth |
| HL | Wakefield | Sheffield | Portsmouth |
| HM | East Ham | Central London | Portsmouth |
| HN | Darlington | Middlesbrough | Portsmouth |
| HO | Hampshire | Bournemouth | Portsmouth |
| HP | Coventry | Coventry | Portsmouth |
| HR | Wiltshire | Swindon | Portsmouth |
| HS | Renfrewshire | Glasgow | Portsmouth |
| HT | Bristol | Bristol | Portsmouth |
| HU | Bristol | Bristol | Portsmouth |
| HV | East Ham | Central London | Portsmouth |
| HW | Bristol | Bristol | Isle of Wight |
| HX | Middlesex | Central London | Portsmouth |
| HY | Bristol | Bristol | Portsmouth |
| HZ | Tyrone | – | – |
| IA | Antrim | Belfast | – |
| IB | Armagh | Belfast | – |
| IC | Carlow | – | – |
| ID | Cavan | – | – |
| IE | Clare | – | – |
| IF | Cork | – | – |
| IH | Donegal | – | – |
| IJ | Down | Belfast | – |
| IK | Dublin | – | – |
| IL | Fermanagh | Belfast | – |
| IM | Galway | – | – |
| IN | Kerry | – | – |
| IO | Kildare | – | – |
| IP | Kilkenny | – | – |
| IR | Offaly | – | – |
| IT | Leitrim | – | – |
| IU | Limerick | – | – |
| IW | Londonderry | Belfast | – |
| IX | Longford | – | – |
| IY | Louth | – | – |
| IZ | Mayo | – | – |
| J | Durham | – | – |
| J | Jersey | Jersey | – |
| JA | Stockport | Manchester | – |
| JB | Berkshire | Reading | – |
| JC | Caernarvonshire | Bangor | – |
| JD | West Ham | Central London | – |
| JE | Isle of Ely | Peterborough | – |
| JF | Leicester | Leicester | – |
| JG | Canterbury | Maidstone | – |
| JH | Hertfordshire | Reading | – |
| JI | Tyrone | Belfast | – |
| JJ | London | Maidstone | – |
| JK | Eastbourne | Brighton | – |
| JL | Lincolnshire | Lincoln | – |
| JM | Westmorland | Reading | – |
| JN | Southend | Chelmsford | – |
| JO | Oxford | Oxford | – |
| JP | Wigan | Liverpool | – |
| JR | Northumberland | Newcastle-upon-Tyne | – |
| JS | Ross and Cromarty | Inverness | – |
| JT | Dorset | Bournemouth | – |
| JU | Leicestershire | Leicester | – |
| JV | Grimsby | Lincoln | – |
| JW | Wolverhampton | Birmingham | – |
| JX | Halifax | Huddersfield | – |
| JY | Plymouth | Exeter | – |
| JZ | Down | – | – |
| K | Liverpool | – | – |
| KA | Liverpool | Liverpool | Luton |
| KB | Liverpool | Liverpool | Luton |
| KC | Liverpool | Liverpool | Luton |
| KD | Liverpool | Liverpool | Luton |
| KE | Kent | Maidstone | Luton |
| KF | Liverpool | Liverpool | Luton |
| KG | Cardiff | Cardiff | Luton |
| KH | Kingston-upon-Hull | Kingston-upon-Hull | Luton |
| KI | Waterford | – | – |
| KJ | Kent | Maidstone | Luton |
| KK | Kent | Maidstone | Luton |
| KL | Kent | Maidstone | Luton |
| KM | Kent | Maidstone | Northampton |
| KN | Kent | Maidstone | Northampton |
| KO | Kent | Maidstone | Northampton |
| KP | Kent | Maidstone | Northampton |
| KR | Kent | Maidstone | Northampton |
| KS | Roxburghshire | Edinburgh | Northampton |
| KT | Kent | Maidstone | Northampton |
| KU | Bradford | Sheffield | Northampton |
| KV | Coventry | Coventry | Northampton |
| KW | Bradford | Sheffield | Northampton |
| KX | Buckinghamshire | Luton | Northampton |
| KY | Bradford | Sheffield | Northampton |
| KZ | Antrim | – | – |
| L | Glamorgan | – | – |
| LA | London | North West London | Wimbledon |
| LB | London | North West London | Wimbledon |
| LC | London | North West London | Wimbledon |
| LD | London | North West London | Wimbledon |
| LE | London | North West London | Wimbledon |
| LF | London | North West London | Wimbledon |
| LG | Cheshire | Chester | Wimbledon |
| LH | London | North West London | Wimbledon |
| LI | Westmeath | – | – |
| LJ | Bournemouth | Bournemouth | Wimbledon |
| LK | London | North West London | Stanmore |
| LL | London | North West London | Stanmore |
| LM | London | North West London | Stanmore |
| LN | London | North West London | Stanmore |
| LO | London | North West London | Stanmore |
| LP | London | North West London | Stanmore |
| LR | London | North West London | Stanmore |
| LS | Selkirk | Edinburgh | Stanmore |
| LT | London | North West London | Stanmore |
| LU | London | North West London | Sidcup |
| LV | Liverpool | Liverpool | Sidcup |
| LW | London | North West London | Sidcup |
| LX | London | North West London | Sidcup |
| LY | London | North West London | Sidcup |
| LZ | Armagh | – | – |
| M | Cheshire | – | – |
| MA | Cheshire | Chester | Manchester |
| MAN | Isle of Man | Isle of Man | |
| MB | Cheshire | Chester | Manchester |
| MC | Middlesex | North East London | Manchester |
| MD | Middlesex | North East London | Manchester |
| ME | Middlesex | North East London | Manchester |
| MF | Middlesex | North East London | Manchester |
| MG | Middlesex | North East London | Manchester |
| MH | Middlesex | North East London | Manchester |
| MI | Wexford | – | – |
| MJ | Bedfordshire | Luton | Manchester |
| MK | Middlesex | North East London | Manchester |
| ML | Middlesex | North East London | Manchester |
| MM | Middlesex | North East London | Manchester |

| | Pre 1974 | 1974 to 2001 | September 2001 onwards |
|---|---|---|---|
| MN | Isle of Man | Isle of Man | Isle of Man |
| MO | Berkshire | Reading | Manchester |
| MP | Middlesex | North East London | Manchester |
| MR | Wiltshire | Swindon | Manchester |
| MS | Stirlingshire | Edinburgh | Manchester |
| MT | Middlesex | North East London | Manchester |
| MU | Middlesex | North East London | Manchester |
| MV | Middlesex | South East London | Manchester |
| MW | Wiltshire | Swindon | Manchester |
| MX | Middlesex | South East London | Manchester |
| MY | Middlesex | South East London | Manchester |
| MZ | Belfast | – | – |
| N | Manchester | – | – |
| NA | Manchester | Manchester | Newcastle-upon-Tyne |
| NB | Manchester | Manchester | Newcastle-upon-Tyne |
| NC | Manchester | Manchester | Newcastle-upon-Tyne |
| ND | Manchester | Manchester | Newcastle-upon-Tyne |
| NE | Manchester | Manchester | Newcastle-upon-Tyne |
| NF | Manchester | Manchester | Newcastle-upon-Tyne |
| NG | Norfolk | Norwich | Newcastle-upon-Tyne |
| NH | Northampton | Northampton | Newcastle-upon-Tyne |
| NI | Wicklow | – | |
| NJ | East Sussex | Brighton | Newcastle-upon-Tyne |
| NK | Hertfordshire | Luton | Newcastle-upon-Tyne |
| NL | Northumberland | Newcastle-upon-Tyne | Newcastle-upon-Tyne |
| NM | Bedfordshire | Luton | Newcastle-upon-Tyne |
| NN | Nottinghamshire | Nottingham | Newcastle-upon-Tyne |
| NO | Essex | Chelmsford | Newcastle-upon-Tyne |
| NP | Worcestershire | Worcester | Stockton-on-Tees |
| NR | Leicestershire | Leicester | Stockton-on-Tees |
| NS | Sutherland | Glasgow | Stockton-on-Tees |
| NT | Shropshire | Shrewsbury | Stockton-on-Tees |
| NU | Derbyshire | Nottingham | Stockton-on-Tees |
| NV | Northamptonshire | Northampton | Stockton-on-Tees |
| NW | Leeds | Leeds | Stockton-on-Tees |
| NX | Warwickshire | Dudley | Stockton-on-Tees |
| NY | Glamorgan | Cardiff | Stockton-on-Tees |
| NZ | Londonderry | – | – |
| O | Birmingham | – | – |
| OA | Birmingham | Birmingham | Oxford |
| OB | Birmingham | Birmingham | Oxford |
| OC | Birmingham | Birmingham | Oxford |
| OD | Devon | Exeter | Oxford |
| OE | Birmingham | Birmingham | Oxford |
| OF | Birmingham | Birmingham | Oxford |
| OG | Birmingham | Birmingham | Oxford |
| OH | Birmingham | Birmingham | Oxford |
| OI | Belfast | Belfast | – |
| OJ | Birmingham | Birmingham | Oxford |
| OK | Birmingham | Birmingham | Oxford |
| OL | Birmingham | Birmingham | Oxford |
| OM | Birmingham | Birmingham | Oxford |
| ON | Birmingham | Birmingham | Oxford |
| OO | Essex | Chelmsford | Oxford |
| OP | Birmingham | Birmingham | Oxford |
| OR | Hampshire | Portsmouth | Oxford |
| OS | Wigtownshire | Glasgow | Oxford |
| OT | Hampshire | Portsmouth | Oxford |
| OU | Hampshire | Bristol | Oxford |
| OV | Birmingham | Birmingham | Oxford |
| OW | Southampton | Portsmouth | Oxford |
| OX | Birmingham | Birmingham | Oxford |
| OY | Croydon | North West London | Oxford |
| OZ | Belfast | – | – |
| P | Surrey | – | – |
| PA | Surrey | Guildford | Preston |
| PB | Surrey | Guildford | Preston |
| PC | Surrey | Guildford | Preston |
| PD | Surrey | Guildford | Preston |
| PE | Surrey | Guildford | Preston |
| PF | Surrey | Guildford | Preston |
| PG | Surrey | Guildford | Preston |
| PH | Surrey | Guildford | Preston |
| PI | Cork | – | – |
| PJ | Surrey | Guildford | Preston |
| PK | Surrey | Guildford | Preston |
| PL | Surrey | Guildford | Preston |
| PM | East Sussex | Guildford | Preston |
| PN | East Sussex | Brighton | Preston |
| PO | West Sussex | Portsmouth | Preston |
| PP | Buckinghamshire | Luton | Preston |
| PR | Dorset | Bournemouth | Preston |

| | Pre 1974 | 1974 to 2001 | September 2001 onwards |
|---|---|---|---|
| PS | Shetland | Aberdeen | Preston |
| PT | Durham | Newcastle-upon-Tyne | Preston |
| PU | Essex | Chelmsford | Carlisle |
| PV | Ipswich | Ipswich | Carlisle |
| PW | Norfolk | Norwich | Carlisle |
| PX | West Sussex | Portsmouth | Carlisle |
| PY | North Yorkshire | Middlesbrough | Carlisle |
| PZ | Belfast | – | – |
| R | Derbyshire | – | – |
| RA | Derbyshire | Nottingham | Reading |
| RB | Derbyshire | Nottingham | Reading |
| RC | Derby | Nottingham | Reading |
| RD | Reading | Reading | Reading |
| RE | Staffordshire | Stoke-on-Trent | Reading |
| RF | Staffordshire | Stoke-on-Trent | Reading |
| RG | Aberdeen | Newcastle-upon-Tyne | Reading |
| RH | Kingston-upon-Hull | Kingston-upon-Hull | Reading |
| RI | Dublin | – | – |
| RJ | Salford | Manchester | Reading |
| RK | Croydon | North West London | Reading |
| RL | Cornwall | Truro | Reading |
| RM | Cumberland | Carlisle | Reading |
| RN | Preston | Preston | Reading |
| RO | Hertfordshire | Luton | Reading |
| RP | Northamptonshire | Northampton | Reading |
| RR | Nottinghamshire | Nottingham | Reading |
| RS | Aberdeen | Aberdeen | Reading |
| RT | East Suffolk | Ipswich | Reading |
| RU | Bournemouth | Bournemouth | Reading |
| RV | Portsmouth | Portsmouth | Reading |
| RW | Coventry | Coventry | Reading |
| RX | Berkshire | Reading | Reading |
| RY | Leicester | Leicester | Reading |
| RZ | Antrim | – | – |
| S | Edinburgh | – | – |
| SA | Aberdeen | Aberdeen | Glasgow |
| SB | Argyllshire | Glasgow | Glasgow |
| SC | Edinburgh | Edinburgh | Glasgow |
| SD | Ayrshire | Glasgow | Glasgow |
| SE | Banffshire | Aberdeen | Glasgow |
| SF | Edinburgh | Edinburgh | Glasgow |
| SG | Edinburgh | Edinburgh | Glasgow |
| SH | Berwickshire | Edinburgh | Glasgow |
| SJ | Bute | Glasgow | Glasgow |
| SK | Caithness | Inverness | Edinburgh |
| SL | Clackmannanshire | Dundee | Edinburgh |
| SM | Dumfriess | Carlisle | Edinburgh |
| SN | Dunbarton | Dundee | Edinburgh |
| SO | Morayshire | Aberdeen | Edinburgh |
| SP | Fifeshire | Dundee | Dundee |
| SR | Angus | Dundee | Dundee |
| SS | East Lothian | Aberdeen | Dundee |
| ST | Inverness | Inverness | Dundee |
| SU | Kincardine | Glasgow | Aberdeen |
| SV | Kinross | – | Aberdeen |
| SW | Kirkcudbright | Carlisle | Aberdeen |
| SX | West Lothian | Edinburgh | Inverness |
| SY | Midlothian | – | Inverness |
| SZ | Down | – | – |
| T | Devon | – | – |
| TA | Devon | Exeter | – |
| TB | Lancashire | Liverpool | – |
| TC | Lancashire | Bristol | – |
| TD | Lancashire | Manchester | – |
| TE | Lancashire | Manchester | – |
| TF | Lancashire | Reading | – |
| TG | Glamorgan | Cardiff | – |
| TH | Carmarthen | Swansea | – |
| TI | Limerick | – | – |
| TJ | Lancashire | Liverpool | – |
| TK | Dorset | Exeter | – |
| TL | Lincolnshire | Lincoln | – |
| TM | Bedfordshire | Luton | – |
| TN | Newcastle-upon-Tyne | Newcastle-upon-Tyne | – |
| TO | Nottingham | Nottingham | – |
| TP | Portsmouth | Portsmouth | – |
| TR | Southampton | Portsmouth | – |
| TS | Dundee | Dundee | – |
| TT | Devon | Exeter | – |
| TU | Cheshire | Chester | – |
| TV | Nottingham | Nottingham | – |
| TW | Essex | Chelmsford | – |

| | Pre 1974 | 1974 to 2001 | September 2001 onwards |
|---|---|---|---|
| TX | Glamorgan | Cardiff | – |
| TY | Northumberland | Newcastle-upon-Tyne | – |
| TZ | Belfast | – | – |
| U | Leeds | – | – |
| UA | Leeds | Leeds | – |
| UB | Leeds | Leeds | – |
| UC | London | Central London | – |
| UD | Oxfordshire | Oxford | – |
| UE | Warwickshire | Dudley | – |
| UF | Brighton | Brighton | – |
| UG | Leeds | Leeds | – |
| UH | Cardiff | Cardiff | – |
| UI | Londonderry | Belfast | – |
| UJ | Shropshire | Shrewsbury | – |
| UK | Wolverhampton | Birmingham | – |
| UL | London | Central London | – |
| UM | Leeds | Leeds | – |
| UN | Denbighshire | Exeter | – |
| UO | Devon | Exeter | – |
| UP | Durham | Newcastle-upon-Tyne | – |
| UR | Hertfordshire | Luton | – |
| US | Glasgow | Glasgow | – |
| UT | Leicestershire | Leicester | – |
| UU | London | Central London | – |
| UV | London | Central London | – |
| UW | London | Central London | – |
| UX | Shropshire | Shrewsbury | – |
| UY | Worcestershire | Worcester | – |
| UZ | Belfast | – | – |
| V | Lanarkshire | – | – |
| VA | Lanarkshire | Peterborough | Worcester |
| VB | Croydon | Maidstone | Worcester |
| VC | Coventry | Coventry | Worcester |
| VD | Lanarkshire | – | Worcester |
| VE | Cambridgeshire | Peterborough | Worcester |
| VF | Norfolk | Norwich | Worcester |
| VG | Norwich | Norwich | Worcester |
| VH | Huddersfield | Huddersfield | Worcester |
| VJ | Herefordshire | Gloucester | Worcester |
| VK | Newcastle-upon-Tyne | Newcastle-upon-Tyne | Worcester |
| VL | Lincoln | Lincoln | Worcester |
| VM | Manchester | Manchester | Worcester |
| VN | North Yorkshire | Middlesbrough | Worcester |
| VO | Nottinghamshire | Nottingham | Worcester |
| VP | Birmingham | Birmingham | Worcester |
| VR | Manchester | Manchester | Worcester |
| VS | Greenock | Luton | Worcester |
| VT | Stoke-on-Trent | Stoke-on-Trent | Worcester |
| VU | Manchester | Manchester | Worcester |
| VV | Northampton | Northampton | Worcester |
| VW | Essex | Chelmsford | Worcester |
| VX | Essex | Chelmsford | Worcester |
| VY | York | Leeds | Worcester |
| VZ | Tyrone | – | – |
| W | Sheffield | – | – |
| WA | Sheffield | Sheffield | Exeter |
| WB | Sheffield | Sheffield | Exeter |
| WC | Essex | Chelmsford | Exeter |
| WD | Warwickshire | Dudley | Exeter |
| WE | Sheffield | Sheffield | Exeter |
| WF | East Yorkshire | Sheffield | Exeter |
| WG | Stirlingshire | Sheffield | Exeter |
| WH | Bolton | Manchester | Exeter |
| WI | Waterford | – | – |
| WJ | Sheffield | Sheffield | Exeter |
| WK | Coventry | Coventry | Truro |
| WL | Oxford | Oxford | Truro |
| WM | Southport | Liverpool | Bristol |
| WN | Swansea | Swansea | Bristol |
| WO | Monmouthshire | Cardiff | Bristol |
| WP | Worcestershire | Worcester | Bristol |
| WR | West Yorkshire | Leeds | Bristol |
| WS | Edinburgh | Bristol | Bristol |
| WT | West Yorkshire | Leeds | Bristol |
| WU | West Yorkshire | Leeds | Bristol |
| WV | Wiltshire | Brighton | Bristol |
| WW | West Yorkshire | Leeds | Bristol |
| WX | West Yorkshire | Leeds | Bristol |
| WY | West Yorkshire | Leeds | Bristol |
| WZ | Belfast | – | – |
| X | Northumberland | – | – |
| XA | London | – | – |

| | Pre 1974 | 1974 to 2001 | September 2001 onwards |
|---|---|---|---|
| XB | London | – | – |
| XC | London | – | – |
| XD | London | – | – |
| XE | London | – | – |
| XF | London | – | – |
| XG | Middlesbrough | – | – |
| XH | London | – | – |
| XI | Belfast | Belfast | – |
| XJ | Manchester | – | – |
| XK | London | – | – |
| XL | London | – | – |
| XM | London | – | – |
| XN | London | – | – |
| XO | London | – | – |
| XP | London | – | – |
| XR | London | – | – |
| XS | Paisley | – | – |
| XT | London | – | – |
| XU | London | – | – |
| XV | London | – | – |
| XW | London | – | – |
| XX | London | – | – |
| XY | London | – | – |
| XZ | Armagh | – | – |
| Y | Somerset | – | – |
| YA | Somerset | Taunton | Leeds |
| YB | Somerset | Taunton | Leeds |
| YC | Somerset | Taunton | Leeds |
| YD | Somerset | Taunton | Leeds |
| YE | London | Central London | Leeds |
| YF | London | Central London | Leeds |
| YG | West Yorkshire | Leeds | Leeds |
| YH | London | Central London | Leeds |
| YI | Dublin | – | – |
| YJ | Dundee | Brighton | Leeds |
| YK | London | Central London | Leeds |
| YL | London | Central London | Sheffield |
| YM | London | Central London | Sheffield |
| YN | London | Central London | Sheffield |
| YO | London | Central London | Sheffield |
| YP | London | Central London | Sheffield |
| YR | London | Central London | Sheffield |
| YS | Glasgow | Glasgow | Sheffield |
| YT | London | Central London | Sheffield |
| YU | London | Central London | Sheffield |
| YV | London | Central London | Beverley |
| YW | London | Central London | Beverley |
| YX | London | Central London | Beverley |
| YY | London | Central London | Beverley |
| YZ | Londonderry | – | – |
| Z | Dublin | – | – |
| ZA | Dublin | – | – |
| ZB | Cork | – | – |
| ZC | Dublin | – | – |
| ZD | Dublin | – | – |
| ZE | Dublin | – | – |
| ZF | Cork | – | – |
| ZH | Dublin | – | – |
| ZI | Dublin | – | – |
| ZJ | Dublin | – | – |
| ZK | Cork | – | – |
| ZL | Dublin | – | – |
| ZM | Galway | – | – |
| ZN | Meath | – | – |
| ZO | Dublin | – | – |
| ZP | Donegal | – | – |
| ZR | Wexford | – | – |
| ZT | Cork | – | – |
| ZU | Dublin | – | – |
| ZW | Kildare | – | – |
| ZX | Kerry | – | – |
| ZY | Louth | – | – |
| ZZ | Dublin | – | – |

# UK Distance Table

| | LONDON | Aberdeen | Aberystwyth | Birmingham | Bournemouth | Brighton | Bristol | Cambridge | Cardiff | Carlisle | Chester | Derby | Dover | Edinburgh | Exeter | Fishguard | Fort William | Glasgow | Harwich | Holyhead |
|---|---|---|---|---|---|---|---|---|---|---|---|---|---|---|---|---|---|---|---|---|
| LONDON | | 806 | 341 | 179 | 169 | 89 | 183 | 84 | 249 | 484 | 298 | 198 | 117 | 608 | 275 | 422 | 818 | 634 | 114 | 420 |
| Aberdeen | 501 | | 724 | 658 | 903 | 895 | 789 | 742 | 792 | 349 | 571 | 634 | 924 | 198 | 911 | 795 | 254 | 241 | 848 | 692 |
| Aberystwyth | 212 | 450 | | 193 | 328 | 425 | 206 | 354 | 177 | 375 | 153 | 222 | 459 | 526 | 325 | 90 | 708 | 525 | 460 | 182 |
| Birmingham | 111 | 409 | 120 | | 237 | 267 | 132 | 161 | 163 | 309 | 117 | 63 | 296 | 460 | 259 | 283 | 642 | 459 | 267 | 246 |
| Bournemouth | 105 | 561 | 204 | 147 | | 148 | 124 | 251 | 195 | 554 | 351 | 306 | 278 | 705 | 132 | 375 | 887 | 703 | 283 | 463 |
| Brighton | 55 | 556 | 264 | 166 | 92 | | 217 | 180 | 288 | 573 | 386 | 286 | 130 | 697 | 275 | 468 | 906 | 723 | 203 | 509 |
| Bristol | 114 | 490 | 128 | 82 | 77 | 135 | | 233 | 71 | 439 | 237 | 195 | 314 | 591 | 121 | 251 | 722 | 589 | 314 | 340 |
| Cambridge | 52 | 461 | 220 | 100 | 156 | 112 | 145 | | 290 | 417 | 269 | 155 | 204 | 544 | 351 | 436 | 750 | 566 | 106 | 391 |
| Cardiff | 155 | 492 | 110 | 101 | 121 | 179 | 44 | 180 | | 443 | 237 | 225 | 385 | 587 | 192 | 180 | 776 | 608 | 359 | 341 |
| Carlisle | 301 | 217 | 233 | 192 | 344 | 356 | 273 | 259 | 275 | | 222 | 304 | 602 | 151 | 571 | 444 | 333 | 150 | 523 | 341 |
| Chester | 185 | 355 | 95 | 73 | 218 | 240 | 147 | 167 | 147 | 138 | | 114 | 415 | 373 | 357 | 243 | 555 | 372 | 375 | 137 |
| Derby | 123 | 394 | 138 | 39 | 190 | 178 | 121 | 96 | 140 | 189 | 71 | | 315 | 436 | 315 | 312 | 637 | 454 | 261 | 251 |
| Dover | 73 | 574 | 285 | 184 | 173 | 81 | 195 | 127 | 239 | 374 | 258 | 196 | | 726 | 391 | 539 | 935 | 752 | 203 | 538 |
| Edinburgh | 378 | 123 | 327 | 286 | 438 | 433 | 367 | 338 | 365 | 94 | 232 | 271 | 451 | | 723 | 616 | 233 | 72 | 650 | 489 |
| Exeter | 171 | 566 | 202 | 161 | 82 | 171 | 75 | 218 | 119 | 355 | 222 | 196 | 243 | 449 | | 372 | 904 | 721 | 389 | 460 |
| Fishguard | 262 | 494 | 56 | 176 | 233 | 291 | 156 | 271 | 112 | 276 | 151 | 194 | 335 | 383 | 231 | | 777 | 594 | 533 | 272 |
| Fort William | 508 | 158 | 440 | 399 | 551 | 563 | 480 | 466 | 482 | 207 | 345 | 396 | 581 | 145 | 562 | 483 | | 183 | 856 | 671 |
| Glasgow | 394 | 150 | 326 | 285 | 437 | 449 | 366 | 352 | 378 | 93 | 231 | 282 | 467 | 45 | 448 | 369 | 114 | | 673 | 488 |
| Harwich | 71 | 527 | 286 | 166 | 176 | 126 | 195 | 66 | 223 | 325 | 233 | 162 | 126 | 404 | 242 | 331 | 532 | 418 | | 497 |
| Holyhead | 261 | 430 | 113 | 153 | 288 | 316 | 211 | 243 | 212 | 212 | 85 | 156 | 334 | 304 | 286 | 169 | 417 | 303 | 309 | |
| Hull | 168 | 348 | 229 | 143 | 255 | 223 | 226 | 124 | 244 | 155 | 132 | 98 | 251 | 225 | 301 | 285 | 362 | 250 | 181 | 217 |
| Inverness | 537 | 105 | 482 | 445 | 594 | 590 | 528 | 497 | 524 | 253 | 387 | 430 | 601 | 159 | 603 | 529 | 66 | 176 | 563 | 463 |
| Leeds | 190 | 322 | 173 | 111 | 261 | 251 | 206 | 148 | 212 | 115 | 78 | 74 | 269 | 199 | 268 | 229 | 322 | 210 | 214 | 163 |
| Leicester | 98 | 417 | 151 | 39 | 166 | 153 | 112 | 68 | 139 | 208 | 94 | 28 | 171 | 294 | 187 | 207 | 415 | 301 | 134 | 183 |
| Lincoln | 136 | 382 | 186 | 85 | 217 | 191 | 163 | 86 | 190 | 180 | 123 | 51 | 213 | 259 | 238 | 245 | 387 | 273 | 152 | 208 |
| Liverpool | 205 | 334 | 104 | 94 | 235 | 260 | 164 | 184 | 164 | 116 | 17 | 88 | 278 | 210 | 239 | 160 | 323 | 211 | 250 | 94 |
| Manchester | 192 | 332 | 133 | 81 | 228 | 247 | 167 | 154 | 172 | 115 | 38 | 58 | 265 | 209 | 242 | 189 | 322 | 210 | 220 | 123 |
| Newcastle | 271 | 230 | 270 | 209 | 348 | 326 | 295 | 231 | 310 | 58 | 175 | 164 | 344 | 107 | 370 | 326 | 257 | 143 | 297 | 260 |
| Norwich | 107 | 487 | 267 | 155 | 212 | 162 | 221 | 60 | 237 | 287 | 210 | 139 | 169 | 364 | 277 | 331 | 494 | 380 | 63 | 299 |
| Nottingham | 123 | 388 | 154 | 50 | 189 | 178 | 132 | 84 | 152 | 185 | 87 | 16 | 196 | 265 | 207 | 210 | 392 | 278 | 150 | 172 |
| Oxford | 56 | 464 | 157 | 62 | 92 | 99 | 66 | 79 | 107 | 256 | 128 | 98 | 129 | 341 | 139 | 207 | 461 | 340 | 134 | 202 |
| Penzance | 282 | 683 | 313 | 268 | 193 | 269 | 186 | 329 | 230 | 466 | 333 | 307 | 354 | 560 | 111 | 342 | 673 | 559 | 353 | 397 |
| Plymouth | 213 | 614 | 244 | 199 | 124 | 213 | 117 | 260 | 161 | 397 | 264 | 238 | 285 | 491 | 42 | 273 | 604 | 490 | 284 | 328 |
| Preston | 216 | 302 | 144 | 105 | 256 | 271 | 185 | 198 | 190 | 85 | 49 | 100 | 289 | 179 | 266 | 200 | 292 | 180 | 264 | 125 |
| Sheffield | 162 | 358 | 158 | 75 | 227 | 217 | 163 | 124 | 176 | 145 | 78 | 36 | 235 | 235 | 248 | 214 | 352 | 240 | 190 | 163 |
| Southampton | 79 | 530 | 202 | 128 | 32 | 60 | 75 | 136 | 119 | 322 | 194 | 164 | 149 | 416 | 111 | 231 | 520 | 415 | 150 | 283 |
| Stranraer | 410 | 235 | 342 | 301 | 453 | 465 | 382 | 368 | 384 | 109 | 247 | 298 | 483 | 133 | 464 | 385 | 199 | 85 | 434 | 321 |
| Swansea | 196 | 506 | 76 | 126 | 162 | 220 | 85 | 216 | 41 | 289 | 151 | 165 | 280 | 383 | 160 | 71 | 496 | 382 | 264 | 189 |
| Worcester | 114 | 428 | 98 | 26 | 131 | 168 | 60 | 116 | 75 | 211 | 88 | 65 | 187 | 305 | 135 | 155 | 418 | 304 | 182 | 152 |
| York | 196 | 309 | 197 | 134 | 273 | 251 | 215 | 157 | 242 | 116 | 102 | 89 | 269 | 186 | 290 | 253 | 323 | 211 | 223 | 187 |

**MILES**

# KILOMETRES

| Hull | Inverness | Leeds | Leicester | Lincoln | Liverpool | Manchester | Newcastle | Norwich | Nottingham | Oxford | Penzance | Plymouth | Preston | Sheffield | Southampton | Stranraer | Swansea | Worcester | York | |
|---|---|---|---|---|---|---|---|---|---|---|---|---|---|---|---|---|---|---|---|---|
| 270 | 864 | 306 | 158 | 219 | 330 | 309 | 436 | 172 | 198 | 90 | 454 | 343 | 348 | 261 | 127 | 660 | 315 | 183 | 315 | **LONDON** |
| 560 | 169 | 518 | 671 | 615 | 538 | 534 | 370 | 784 | 624 | 747 | 1099 | 988 | 486 | 576 | 853 | 378 | 814 | 689 | 497 | Aberdeen |
| 369 | 776 | 278 | 243 | 304 | 167 | 214 | 435 | 430 | 248 | 253 | 504 | 393 | 232 | 254 | 325 | 550 | 122 | 148 | 317 | Aberystwyth |
| 230 | 716 | 179 | 63 | 137 | 151 | 130 | 336 | 249 | 80 | 100 | 431 | 320 | 169 | 121 | 206 | 484 | 203 | 42 | 216 | Birmingham |
| 410 | 956 | 420 | 267 | 349 | 378 | 367 | 560 | 341 | 304 | 148 | 311 | 200 | 412 | 365 | 51 | 729 | 261 | 211 | 439 | Bournemouth |
| 359 | 950 | 404 | 246 | 307 | 418 | 398 | 525 | 261 | 286 | 159 | 433 | 343 | 436 | 349 | 97 | 748 | 354 | 270 | 404 | Brighton |
| 364 | 850 | 332 | 180 | 262 | 264 | 269 | 475 | 356 | 212 | 106 | 299 | 188 | 298 | 262 | 121 | 615 | 137 | 97 | 346 | Bristol |
| 200 | 800 | 238 | 109 | 138 | 296 | 248 | 372 | 97 | 135 | 127 | 529 | 418 | 319 | 200 | 219 | 592 | 348 | 187 | 253 | Cambridge |
| 393 | 843 | 341 | 224 | 306 | 264 | 277 | 499 | 381 | 245 | 172 | 370 | 259 | 306 | 283 | 192 | 618 | 66 | 121 | 389 | Cardiff |
| 249 | 407 | 185 | 335 | 290 | 187 | 185 | 93 | 462 | 298 | 412 | 750 | 639 | 137 | 233 | 518 | 175 | 465 | 340 | 187 | Carlisle |
| 212 | 623 | 126 | 151 | 198 | 27 | 61 | 282 | 338 | 140 | 206 | 536 | 425 | 79 | 126 | 312 | 398 | 243 | 142 | 164 | Chester |
| 158 | 692 | 119 | 45 | 82 | 142 | 93 | 264 | 224 | 26 | 158 | 494 | 383 | 161 | 58 | 264 | 480 | 266 | 105 | 143 | Derby |
| 404 | 967 | 433 | 275 | 343 | 447 | 426 | 554 | 272 | 315 | 208 | 570 | 459 | 465 | 378 | 240 | 777 | 451 | 301 | 433 | Dover |
| 362 | 256 | 320 | 473 | 417 | 338 | 336 | 172 | 586 | 426 | 549 | 901 | 790 | 288 | 378 | 669 | 214 | 616 | 491 | 299 | Edinburgh |
| 484 | 970 | 431 | 301 | 383 | 385 | 389 | 595 | 446 | 333 | 224 | 179 | 68 | 428 | 399 | 179 | 747 | 257 | 217 | 467 | Exeter |
| 459 | 851 | 369 | 333 | 394 | 257 | 304 | 525 | 533 | 338 | 333 | 550 | 439 | 322 | 344 | 372 | 620 | 114 | 429 | 407 | Fishguard |
| 583 | 106 | 518 | 668 | 623 | 520 | 518 | 414 | 795 | 631 | 742 | 1083 | 972 | 470 | 566 | 837 | 320 | 798 | 673 | 520 | Fort William |
| 402 | 283 | 338 | 484 | 439 | 340 | 338 | 230 | 612 | 447 | 547 | 900 | 789 | 290 | 386 | 668 | 137 | 615 | 489 | 340 | Glasgow |
| 291 | 906 | 344 | 216 | 245 | 402 | 354 | 478 | 101 | 241 | 216 | 568 | 457 | 425 | 306 | 241 | 698 | 429 | 293 | 359 | Harwich |
| 349 | 745 | 262 | 295 | 335 | 151 | 198 | 418 | 481 | 277 | 325 | 639 | 528 | 201 | 262 | 455 | 517 | 304 | 245 | 301 | Holyhead |
|  | 615 | 90 | 145 | 61 | 196 | 151 | 190 | 240 | 148 | 262 | 663 | 552 | 180 | 103 | 412 | 425 | 433 | 272 | 63 | Hull |
| 382 |  | 579 | 729 | 673 | 605 | 604 | 428 | 842 | 682 | 816 | 1159 | 1049 | 555 | 634 | 925 | 417 | 872 | 747 | 552 | Inverness |
| 56 | 358 |  | 158 | 108 | 119 | 64 | 148 | 277 | 116 | 272 | 613 | 502 | 90 | 58 | 378 | 360 | 369 | 220 | 39 | Leeds |
| 90 | 453 | 98 |  | 82 | 187 | 138 | 301 | 187 | 42 | 119 | 480 | 369 | 206 | 105 | 225 | 510 | 282 | 109 | 174 | Leicester |
| 38 | 418 | 67 | 51 |  | 192 | 137 | 245 | 169 | 56 | 201 | 562 | 451 | 185 | 72 | 307 | 465 | 340 | 192 | 124 | Lincoln |
| 122 | 376 | 74 | 116 | 119 |  | 55 | 253 | 360 | 167 | 251 | 563 | 452 | 50 | 119 | 357 | 362 | 270 | 169 | 158 | Liverpool |
| 94 | 375 | 40 | 86 | 85 | 34 |  | 212 | 306 | 119 | 230 | 568 | 457 | 48 | 64 | 325 | 360 | 295 | 164 | 103 | Manchester |
| 118 | 266 | 92 | 187 | 152 | 157 | 132 |  | 414 | 254 | 412 | 774 | 663 | 203 | 206 | 518 | 262 | 517 | 378 | 127 | Newcastle |
| 149 | 523 | 174 | 116 | 105 | 224 | 190 | 257 |  | 198 | 224 | 626 | 515 | 354 | 241 | 299 | 637 | 439 | 283 | 293 | Norwich |
| 92 | 424 | 72 | 26 | 35 | 104 | 74 | 158 | 123 |  | 156 | 512 | 401 | 167 | 64 | 262 | 473 | 283 | 122 | 134 | Nottingham |
| 163 | 507 | 169 | 74 | 125 | 156 | 143 | 256 | 139 | 97 |  | 402 | 291 | 272 | 217 | 106 | 587 | 230 | 95 | 291 | Oxford |
| 412 | 720 | 381 | 298 | 349 | 350 | 353 | 481 | 389 | 318 | 250 |  | 126 | 597 | 560 | 357 | 925 | 436 | 396 | 645 | Penzance |
| 343 | 652 | 312 | 229 | 280 | 281 | 284 | 412 | 320 | 249 | 181 | 78 |  | 486 | 447 | 246 | 814 | 325 | 285 | 534 | Plymouth |
| 112 | 345 | 56 | 128 | 115 | 31 | 30 | 126 | 220 | 104 | 169 | 371 | 302 |  | 113 | 375 | 312 | 322 | 203 | 126 | Preston |
| 64 | 394 | 36 | 65 | 45 | 74 | 40 | 128 | 150 | 40 | 135 | 348 | 278 | 70 |  | 323 | 490 | 336 | 163 | 90 | Sheffield |
| 256 | 575 | 235 | 140 | 191 | 222 | 202 | 322 | 186 | 163 | 66 | 222 | 153 | 233 | 201 |  | 679 | 257 | 193 | 398 | Southampton |
| 264 | 259 | 224 | 317 | 289 | 225 | 224 | 163 | 396 | 294 | 365 | 575 | 506 | 194 | 254 | 422 |  | 461 | 515 | 362 | Stranraer |
| 269 | 542 | 229 | 175 | 211 | 168 | 183 | 321 | 273 | 176 | 143 | 271 | 202 | 200 | 209 | 160 | 398 |  | 161 | 418 | Swansea |
| 169 | 464 | 137 | 68 | 119 | 105 | 102 | 235 | 176 | 76 | 59 | 246 | 177 | 126 | 101 | 120 | 320 | 100 |  | 257 | Worcester |
| 39 | 343 | 24 | 108 | 77 | 98 | 64 | 79 | 182 | 83 | 181 | 401 | 332 | 78 | 56 | 247 | 225 | 260 | 160 |  | York |

# Year Planner 2018

| Month | S | S | M | T | W | T | F | S | S | M | T | W | T | F | S | S | M |
|---|---|---|---|---|---|---|---|---|---|---|---|---|---|---|---|---|---|
| January |  |  | 1 | 2 | 3 | 4 | 5 | 6 | 7 | 8 | 9 | 10 | 11 | 12 | 13 | 14 | 15 |
| February |  |  |  |  |  | 1 | 2 | 3 | 4 | 5 | 6 | 7 | 8 | 9 | 10 | 11 | 12 |
| March |  |  |  |  |  | 1 | 2 | 3 | 4 | 5 | 6 | 7 | 8 | 9 | 10 | 11 | 12 |
| April |  | 1 | 2 | 3 | 4 | 5 | 6 | 7 | 8 | 9 | 10 | 11 | 12 | 13 | 14 | 15 | 16 |
| May |  |  |  | 1 | 2 | 3 | 4 | 5 | 6 | 7 | 8 | 9 | 10 | 11 | 12 | 13 | 14 |
| June |  |  |  |  |  |  | 1 | 2 | 3 | 4 | 5 | 6 | 7 | 8 | 9 | 10 | 11 |
| July |  | 1 | 2 | 3 | 4 | 5 | 6 | 7 | 8 | 9 | 10 | 11 | 12 | 13 | 14 | 15 | 16 |
| August |  |  |  |  | 1 | 2 | 3 | 4 | 5 | 6 | 7 | 8 | 9 | 10 | 11 | 12 | 13 |
| September | 1 | 2 | 3 | 4 | 5 | 6 | 7 | 8 | 9 | 10 | 11 | 12 | 13 | 14 | 15 | 16 | 17 |
| October |  |  | 1 | 2 | 3 | 4 | 5 | 6 | 7 | 8 | 9 | 10 | 11 | 12 | 13 | 14 | 15 |
| November |  |  |  |  |  | 1 | 2 | 3 | 4 | 5 | 6 | 7 | 8 | 9 | 10 | 11 | 12 |
| December | 1 | 2 | 3 | 4 | 5 | 6 | 7 | 8 | 9 | 10 | 11 | 12 | 13 | 14 | 15 | 16 | 17 |